THE POWER OF CHANCE

Myself when young

RUPERT HART-DAVIS

The Power of Chance

A TABLE OF MEMORY

Our lives are in the power of chance.
GIBBON

We, that are very old, are better able to
remember things which befell us in our distant
youth, than the passage of later days.
RICHARD STEELE

The gift of total recall is not a gift but a disaster.
ARTHUR MARSHALL

SINCLAIR-STEVENSON

First published in Great Britain by
Sinclair-Stevenson Limited
7/8 Kendrick Mews
London sw7 3hg, England

British Library Cataloguing in Publication Data
A CIP catalogue record for this book is available
from the British Library.
isbn 1 85619 077 3

Typeset by Butler & Tanner Limited
Printed and bound in Great Britain
Butler & Tanner, Frome & London.

This book is dedicated
with very much love
to my three children
and six grandchildren

CONTENTS

ILLUSTRATIONS

INTRODUCTION

IN RECENT years four different men have asked if they could write the story of my life. Surprised but flattered, I firmly refused their requests, knowing how difficult, if not impossible, it would be for any of them to assemble events in the right order, let alone to analyse my memories and feelings. Then, realising that after my death one or more of these intrepid scribes might go ahead, I decided that in self-defence I had better write my own account of all those years.

In my memoir of my mother, *The Arms of Time,* I told all that needs telling of my first nineteen years, and this book, beginning exactly where that one ended, covers my next nineteen.

I hate the huge and heavy biographies of these days, which are difficult to hold or read without a book-rest or lectern, so I have cut my story short at a convenient moment. If I live long enough, the next volume will give some account of my post-war activities as publisher, author and editor.

'Vanity,' wrote Joseph Conrad, 'plays lurid tricks with our memory,' and Enid Bagnold added: 'What one remembers is richer than the thing itself.' I have done my best to avoid vanity and enrichment, so as to deliver what Othello called 'a round unvarnished tale'.

Luckily I kept a daily diary for 1928, 1929 and part of 1931, and sentences in quotation-marks in those years come from there. Otherwise I have had to rely on my memory, on surviving letters, other documents, and biographies of my friends and contemporaries. A few short passages have already appeared in various books and periodicals. If I had included all the people I knew and liked during those years, my narrative would have been clogged by names.

I have taken the advice of the fifth Earl of Orrery, who wrote in 1741: 'I look upon anecdotes as debts due to the public, which every man, when he has that kind of cash by him, ought to pay.'

Writing all this book in my eighties, I have come to appreciate more and more the thundering common sense of Dr Johnson when he wrote:

Composition is, for the most part, an effort of slow diligence and steady perseverance, to which the mind is dragged by necessity or resolution, and from which the attention is every moment starting to more delightful amusements.

But, despite that acute description, I have enjoyed delving into the past and indulging in the remembrance of things long past, and I only hope that my enjoyment will be shared by a few others.

Rupert Hart-Davis

Marske-in-Swaledale

1991

POSTSCRIPT

Since I wrote the above, Dame Peggy Ashcroft, my Peg, has died. She was eighty-three, just four months younger than myself. Although latterly we seldom met, our affection for each other lasted to the end. She had read and approved of everything about her in this book. She was a wonderful person and a great actress.

R. H.-D.

PROLOGUE : SWEEPING UP THE HEART

The bustle in a house
The morning after death
Is solemnest of industries
Enacted upon earth –

The sweeping up the heart,
And putting love away
We shall not want to use again
Until eternity.

EMILY DICKINSON

[1]

MY BELOVED mother died on 3 January 1927. I was nineteen, my sister Deirdre seventeen. Our mother had always been a magical presence to us, the unchanging centre of our life and love. Now we were left dependent on a father with whom we had little in common.

After the funeral at Kensal Green and the requiem mass in St James's, Spanish Place, he took us for a week to a hotel at Sidmouth on the South Devon coast. I'm sure it is a delightful place, but my memory of those dreadful days is of red cliffs seen through a blur of desolation which made any activity impossible, even my favourite occupation, reading.

Then Deirdre returned to the Ozannes' finishing school in Paris, and for the three months of her term we wrote to each other every day.

Meanwhile I took refuge with the Meynell family at Greatham, near Pulborough in Sussex. My mother had always been happy there, and I had accompanied her on one brief visit. Now the family wrapped me in cherishing affection, and very soon I fell in love with all of them, from the patriarchal Wilfrid (widower of the poet Alice), aged seventy-five, through his daughter Viola, poet and novelist, to the youngest grandchild living there, Barbara Lucas.

*Wilfrid Meynell by Anne Brindley
1927*

Wilfrid, as a working journalist, editor and author of books, had known most of the writers of the last fifty years and delighted me with anecdotes about them. He also read poetry beautifully. As Viola wrote of him after his death, 'It was on affection that his character was founded'. Fifteen years later, when I was a serving soldier, Viola's letter, telling me that her father was still mowing the lawn, occasioned the only epigram I have ever written:

> On a prospect of W.M. in his ninetieth year.

> 'Time, you had better put your scythe away.
> Our dearest Wilfrid mows the lawn today.'

But of all that welcoming company I fell most heavily in love with Anne Brindley, an orphan of twenty-seven who was living at Greatham and helping to look after the old man. She and my mother had been devoted to each other, and Anne seemed to be taking my mother's place. I had never been in love before, nor, I fancy, had she. Books and poetry were her great delight; it all seemed fated. Anyhow our affection was mutual, and we decided to get married as soon as possible, and to open a secondhand bookshop. The Meynells applauded.

Early in February I returned to Oxford for my second term. My first one had been ruined by distracting fears for my mother's health, and now I quickly discovered that I was still unable to concentrate. Anne came to visit me and we spent some days together in London. Finally I asked to see the Master of Balliol. A. D. (Sandy) Lindsay was not universally popular, but he was very kind to me. I told him that I proposed to leave Oxford for good at the end of the term. He asked me why, and I told him that there seemed to me only two reasons for being at Oxford – to do some work or to enjoy oneself – and in my present state I was incapable of either. He asked me what I intended to do instead. I hadn't thought as far as that, but on the spur of the moment, remembering how much I had enjoyed the two Shaw plays which Peter Fleming and I had put on in the School Hall at Eton, I said: 'I shall go on the stage'. 'Oh,' said the Master, 'You won't find many Old Balliol men there'. Nor did I.

My father was now doubly incensed. He had always hoped I would join his stockbroking firm, which I would have done anything to avoid, and he refused to acknowledge my engagement to Anne, forbidding me to see her – a prohibition which I quietly ignored.

Our large house in Kent had been sold, and we now rented 25 Ovington Square, off the Brompton Road, for four months. On 14 March 1927 I left Oxford for good – a departure I have never regretted – and went to stay at Greatham. Relations with my father steadily deteriorated, and finally he insisted on my going abroad to learn some languages.

[2]

The *pension* was a grim little house on the outskirts of Fontainebleau. Opposite it was a huge Judas tree in full bloom. My small room looked out over the back garden. A hot bath had to be ordered at least a day in advance. I spent six summer weeks there. My father believed that this enforced separation would bring my romance with Anne to an end, but in fact it almost certainly had the opposite effect. We wrote to each other every day and Anne sent me books.

I did some German with a nice old retired English schoolmaster called Perry: we read Heine's letters, which I found entertaining. I was also supposed to learn Spanish with a retired Alsatian colonel called Armbruster. He was a genial character, full of anecdotes and bawdy stories, but of Spanish I learned almost nothing.

In my spare time I walked alone in the silent, birdless forest, mourning my mother and reciting to the trees some of the poems she loved. Occasionally I would watch the monstrous fish in the castle lake and console myself by eating delicious cakes in a *patisserie*. I read several Hardy novels for the first time.

Every week-end I took a train to Paris, where I stayed in a hotel and went to the theatre with Deirdre and my mother's dear friend Marie Ozanne. We saw plays by Rostand, Giraudoux, and Henry Bernstein, performances by Sacha Guitry, Yvonne Printemps, the Pitoeffs, Charles Dullin, Louis Jouvet and many more. We also enjoyed the Grand Guignol.

I arrived home to discover that my father had acquired a huge four-storey house, 44 Hans Place, behind Harrods. I had a spacious flat on the third floor. Deirdre and I worked hard arranging furniture.

I was still determined to try the stage, and my father reluctantly forked out forty pounds for me to spend a season as a so-called student at the Old Vic. I was told I had to pass an audition by reciting a piece of Shakespeare from the stage. Luckily I possessed a gramophone record of Beerbohm Tree declaiming Antony's speech over Caesar's body, which begins: 'Oh pardon me, thou bleeding piece of earth'. This I learned by heart, with all Tree's stresses and intonations, and I delivered it with some force in the huge, empty and dilapidated theatre, to an audience of two in the stalls – the great boss Lilian Baylis with her lop-sided face and ramshackle clothes, beside a diminutive comedy actor called Andrew Leigh, who was to be the producer (i.e. director) for the season. They told me I had passed, and it was only later that I realised the audition was a farce, since they were finding it almost impossible to recruit any male students, and when the company first assembled the female students outnumbered the men by eight to four.

PART ONE : THE THEATRE

Theatrical reminiscence is the most awful weapon
in the armoury of old age.

MAX BEERBOHM

[1]

ALL ON an August morning we crowded into the large rehearsal room
in the Old Vic: the complete company, the students, the stage manager
and some others. We had been told that, owing to badly needed
redecoration at the Vic, the first four plays of the season would be
presented at the Lyric Theatre, Hammersmith, with Sybil Thorndike
and her husband Lewis Casson in the leading parts. The present
occasion was a read-through of *The Taming of the Shrew,* at which all
sat round, marking their rôles in the little Temple edition of Shakespeare
as they went along: all but Sybil, who had no book, since she knew her
part by heart, and also the part of Lewis, who was bad at learning and
remembering his lines.

All proceeded smoothly until in Act IV Scene 2 the stage-direction
'Enter a pedant' caused shouts of 'Charlie Marford' throughout the
theatre, and eventually there appeared a young-old man with a handsome battered face. He was dressed in very dirty grey flannel trousers
and a long painter's smock covered with multi-coloured paint. He was
roaring with laughter, in which everyone joined, and since he became
one of my dearest friends he must have a section to himself.

[2]

Charlie was born in 1887 at Hackney in the East End of London,
where his father was a baker and pastrycook. The family originally
came from Germany and their name was Mardorf. In 1914 by a silent
transposition of two consonants they changed it to Marford, which had
a solid English ring.

Such schooling as Charlie received from the ages of five to fourteen was at the London Elementary Board School in Stepney, but during those years and for the rest of his life he was self-educated. He was a precocious and fanatical reader, and by the time he was ten he had read five Shakespeare plays. Then he moved on to Dickens, Kingsley and Stevenson, and he spent some time vainly trying to prove that Goldsmith Row, where he lived, was in some way connected with the author of *The Vicar of Wakefield* and *She Stoops to Conquer*.

In his holidays and spare time he did various odd jobs for a few pence, including one as lather-boy in a barber's shop, but his greatest pleasure was to act as errand-boy and labourer for his Uncle Will, who was a professional scene-painter or, as he called it, scenic artist: gradually Charlie became an unpaid apprentice, very accomplished in his uncle's profession.

When he left school he got a job as a junior clerk in a lawyer's office in the City. He found the work boring, but happily spent most of his evenings, week-ends and holidays with amateur and semi-professional players, acting, singing, dancing, stage-managing and scene-painting. His total earnings were less than three pounds a week. Much of this work was done in the East End of London, at the Britannia, Hoxton; the Pavilion, Whitechapel; and the Varieties, Hoxton (locally known as the Sods' Opera). He also frequented Pollock's toy-theatre shop, and was a devoted maker and user of toy-theatres for the rest of his life.

He married in 1907, when he was twenty, and in time fathered five or six children. They lived at Benfleet in Essex and Charlie commuted to London, sometimes by bicycle.

So things continued until August 1914, when Charlie, saying 'You can't be a pacifist in wartime', volunteered for the army.

'What regiment were you in, Charlie?'

'The Ninety-third London, commonly known as the 'Ackney Gur-khas'.

In a training-camp on the south coast he organised a battalion concert-party, which was so successful that in France in 1916 he was put in charge of a divisional concert-party. When they learned that all ranks of the French army were issued with a daily wine-ration, they got lost, joined a French unit, entertained them for some weeks, and, fortified by wine, eventually found their own division again.

Charlie's law-firm had paid his wife half-wages for his army years, and he sent her what he could from his army pay. Miraculously he survived four years of military service without wound or illness.

Charlie Marford by Liza Stillman

After the war the retired actress Lena Ashwell organised a theatrical company for demobilised actors, and Charlie worked for her as stage-manager and scenic artist for three years. They played mostly in municipal halls all over England, and at Scarborough he remembered Charles Laughton as an amateur super paid two shillings a night.

Then he worked for various managers – Herbert Mansfield at Dundee, Ben Greet on tour, and the Birmingham Rep. In one of these jobs he met the actor and designer John Garside, who introduced him to Lilian Baylis, and Charlie worked at the Old Vic from 1924 to 1928. When I met him there in 1927 he was playing small parts (which he called 'spits and coughs') and painting scenery on a huge frame and an adjustable platform. This was an immense task, since Shakespeare was then alternating with opera, the theatre was short of scenery, and Charlie often had to spend the week-end transforming the huge backcloth of the Forest of Arden into Pharaoh's palace for *Aida*.

He had recently decided that, at the age of forty, he couldn't go on applying for parts as a Juvenile. Not wanting to become a 'Heavy' immediately, he covered almost everything by describing himself as Character Juvenile, and since advertisements in the theatrical papers were charged by the inch he simply described himself as CHAS MARFORD CHAR JUV. I often addressed him as Char Juv thereafter.

My father had an old chauffeur who always addressed me and Deirdre as Mr Rudolph and Miss Dreary. Charlie was delighted with this, and he and Molly called me Rudolph for the rest of their lives. Whenever I did Charlie any kindness he always said: "Rudolph, you're a toff".

[3]

In 1918 the actor Nigel Playfair discovered a derelict theatre in a slum. With the help of wealthy friends, including Arnold Bennett, he restored it as a snug Victorian theatre called the Lyric, Hammersmith. Successes such as John Drinkwater's *Abraham Lincoln,* which ran for a year, Gay's *Beggar's Opera,* which ran for three years, and Congreve's *Way of the World,* with Edith Evans as Millamant (158 performances) brought audiences streaming from the West End. To help the Old Vic he leased the theatre to them for their 1927–28 season.

By the time *The Taming of the Shrew* opened there on 12 September I had got to know all the actors: Percy Walsh, the 'heavy' man, who later had a great success as the tutor in Terence Rattigan's *French without Tears*; the diminutive Scottish comedian D. Hay Petrie, who gave brilliant performances as Christopher Sly, Launcelot Gobbo, Dogberry, and Fluellen; a pathetic old actor who spent much of his time giving sweets to little boys on the fire-escape; Maurice Farquharson, who, as assistant stage-manager and actor, was like a warrant officer between officers (the company) and other ranks (the students); and the juvenile lead Eric Portman. When he was engaged to play Romeo, Bassanio, Charles Surface etc, and his salary of a few pounds a week had been agreed, Miss Baylis suddenly asked him:

'Are you pure, dear boy?'

'I beg your pardon, Miss Baylis.'

'I asked you if you were pure.'

'I hope so, Miss Baylis.'

'I'm all for everybody having their proper mate (pronounced mite) in life, but I don't like it going on in the wings.'

Above all my friendship with Charlie Marford had blossomed. He

The Duke of Orleans

Charles Surface

Macmorris

Three characters

was one of the most intelligent and witty people I have known, and his company was always a delight. His wide vocabulary derived from his reading and from old Cockney rhyming and theatre slang with military undertones. At the Lyric we shared a corner of a long dressing-room, which housed six other performers, and there Charlie taught me the rudiments of make-up. His stock of cosmetics consisted of a few stubs of various greasepaints which other actors had found too small to use.

Most of the backstage staff were aspiring or failed artists and writers: the man who let the curtain up and down was experimenting with colour-photography in a barge on the Thames. Our genial dresser Jack had literary aspirations, and whenever we needed him he was usually in some other part of the theatre reading James Joyce's *Ulysses*. After we had been there a week or two he came in one evening and in a loudish stage-whisper announced to Charlie and me: 'There's buggery aboard, sir'. We enjoyed and thanked him for this nautical warning. The stage-doorkeeper George Gamble was a little man with longish hair and an immensely histrionic face, which made him look like a pocket Irving. When at Christmas I gave him a tiny present he wrote me a note of gratitude, in which he said: 'Always follow such generous impulses, dear lad' – a precept which I have tried to follow ever since. The whole place was like a family party.

I found the company of all these disparate characters very stimulating, so different from the uniformity of Eton and Oxford (not a Balliol man in sight), and during my two years on the stage I certainly learned more of life and the world than I would have done in twice the time at a university. Best of all I learned seven Shakespeare plays almost by heart. I had read most of them, but had seen none acted except John Barrymore's impressive Hamlet. Now, taking part in scenes and standing for long hours in the background with my halberd, I absorbed all the matchless words, as I had the words of the Authorised Version of the Bible in Eton Chapel.

In the month's run of *The Shrew* I at various times played huntsman, cook and tailor. In *The Merchant of Venice* I was Portia's servant Stephano, and in *Much Ado* one of Dogberry's watchmen. In *Henry V* I had two tiny parts, each with a few words to say, Macmorris and the Duke of Orleans.

I had seen and greatly admired Sybil Thorndike in *St Joan* and other plays. Now I was able to study her versatility and professionalism as Katharine, Portia, Beatrice and the French Princess at close quarters. Everybody loved her, and at Christmas she gave everyone in the theatre a specially chosen present. Mine was an English translation of *The Tosa Diary*, a tenth-century Japanese classic, which I treasure less for its contents than for Sybil's inscription in it. Her husband Lewis Casson always subordinated himself to Sybil's genius, but he was a fine actor and also an accomplished director. Whenever Andrew Leigh was called away during rehearsal Lewis took over and admirably raised the tempo of the acting.

I was now so busy, every weekday morning rehearsing the next play at the Old Vic in the Waterloo Road, most afternoons trying to learn the parts we were supposed to be understudying, and every evening going across to Hammersmith for a performance, that I had little time to myself and naturally saw little of Anne, who was still at Greatham. Gradually and sadly I came to realise that in those agonising months after my mother died at the beginning of the year I hadn't been looking for a wife or a mistress, but for a mother, and Anne had lovingly adopted that rôle. Now I knew that I didn't want to be married immediately, without any money except a small allowance from my father, and stumblingly I explained this to Anne in the Meynells' London house. She said, bless her, that she had all along been afraid that our romance couldn't last. She was a lovely person. Tearfully we said goodbye to each other. I felt terribly guilty about the whole thing, especially because I was happily embarked on a profession and she had only Greatham to go back to. I never saw her again, but in 1979 I sent her a copy of my memoir of my mother, *The Arms of Time*, and she wrote me a beautiful letter of gratitude and forgiveness. She died in 1983.

[4]

On 14 February 1928 the refurbished Old Vic opened with *Romeo and Juliet*. Sybil and Lewis had been succeeded by Jean Forbes-Robertson and Ernest Milton, both artists *sui generis*, unlike any others. Jean was more like a spirit than a mortal, with her unearthly beauty and individual approach to every rôle. She never seemed to know what the play, or even her own part in it, was about, but she learned her lines assiduously and spoke them with an unfailing instinct, bequeathed to her by her distinguished father. Her Juliet was lovely. She was twenty-three.

Ernest was an experienced actor of thirty-eight. He was small, Jewish, with a fine vocal range and often a hint of the sinister. I had admired his superb performances in Galsworthy's *Loyalties* and Pirandello's *Henry IV*. Now his Mercutio held me in thrall: one critic described it as 'a rare exotic among native fauna'. Apart from standing about and fighting in the crowd-scene I had the tiny part of Romeo's servant Balthasar, who travels to Mantua to tell the banished Romeo of Juliet's supposed death. I loved speaking such lines as:

> 'Her body sleeps in Capels' monument.
> And her immortal part with angels lives.'

After the close-knit cosiness of Hammersmith the backstage regions of the Vic seemed like a cluttered railway station, ruled by the filthy stage-doorkeeper Old Bob, who, with his equally horrible acolyte Nightingale, spied on all the cast, hoping to detect irregularity, immorality or other misdemeanour which they could repeat to Miss Baylis, who was always in close touch with God. The building was infested with very peculiar clergymen, one of whom, Father Andrew, used to seize and kiss any young member of the cast, male or female, whom he could catch. The wardrobe-master Orlando Whitehead was a disagreeable man who disliked all actors and particularly actresses, so that their dressers always had great difficulty in getting the right costumes. Altogether the theatre, backstage, was not a happy place.

Luckily Charlie and I shared a dressing-room. He had fallen in love with a delightful girl called Molly, who had been a student in the previous season. One day he came in wearing much cleaner trousers than usual.

'You're looking very smart today, Charlie.'

'These are me whoring trousers, boy.'

Romeo was followed by *The Two Noble Kinsmen*, a play by John Fletcher, in which some believed Shakespeare had a hand. I could detect little evidence for this, except in the part of the Gaoler's mad daughter, which contains echoes of Ophelia and was beautifully acted by Jean. The plot came from Chaucer's *Knight's Tale*, in which two kinsmen, Palamon and Arcite, swear eternal friendship and then fall in love with the same lady.

The costumes were vaguely Chaucerian, and Ernest, as Palamon, wore a bright red wig which made him resemble a pantomime dame. When he and Eric Portman (Arcite) made their first entrance together the whole audience collapsed in helpless laughter. Ernest had rehearsed in all seriousness, but in a flash he realised that this would no longer do, and he immediately, and for the rest of the run, played the part very successfully as high comedy, a brilliant improvisation. Maurice Farquharson and I were the Gaoler's Friends.

Two days later came one of the most dreaded occasions of the year, an L.C.C. Schoolchildren's matinée. The enormous theatre was filled with seventeen hundred screaming children who wet the seats, plastered the auditorium with toffee and chewing-gum and covered the floor with litter. Every year the cleaning staff threatened to go on strike and had to be appeased with a bonus. In 1927 the noise had drowned the actors' voices, and all headmasters had threatened severe penalties for any child making a sound during the action of the play. Charlie, thinking the silence uncanny, stole through the pass-door into the dress circle. There in the front row he found a little boy bashing his neighbour's head against the brass rail in front of them, occasionally stopping to put his finger to his lips and hiss 'Sh' before continuing his assault.

The Merchant was revived for this jamboree, with Ernest as Shylock. I played Gratiano without a rehearsal.

Two days later Charlie took me and three other men to one of Miss Baylis's charities, the Moorhouse Leper Colony in Essex, which was run by Franciscans. Charlie had done so much for them that they made him a Lay Brother, which he said was the nicest thing that had happened in his life. We put on an unrehearsed concert-party entertainment. Our pianist and Charlie sang songs, Charlie and I acted scenes from Shakespeare – Brutus and Cassius, Shylock and Tubal. I recited some poems and read aloud Oscar Wilde's story 'The Happy Prince'. Charlie did some of his stunt drawings – an elephant, which turned upside down was a caricature of Lloyd George, and so on. The poor lepers loved it all, and it was heartbreaking to watch the enjoyment of these doomed ones. I remember particularly an old blind sea-captain and a little girl.

[5]

It was at this time that I came to know the Jackson family. The father had been head of the Bar in Calcutta, where he was known as Tiger Jackson. Now eighty-six, he had retired to a small villa in the outskirts of Worthing on the Sussex coast. His son Richard Leofric (always called Joe) I remembered as a heavyweight boxer at Eton. He was called to the Bar, worked for years in the Public Prosecutor's office and ended his career as head of the C.I.D. at Scotland Yard.

His sister Yolande was a lovely girl, large and gay and beautiful, full of joy and jokes and friendliness. I was never in love with her but greatly enjoyed her company. She was a student at the Royal Academy of Dramatic Art, where I saw her play some scenes as Hamlet. She had a flat in Manchester Street, where she gave after-the-play parties. I went along with Eric Portman, who though homosexual was her beau of the moment. The parties consisted of four men and four girls, sitting in couples in a dimly-lit room where food and drink were handed round. I was paired off with a most attractive Scottish girl called Marjorie MacIntyre, who was also a R.A.D.A. student. I fell in love with her, and she with me, but her return to Edinburgh parted us, and four years later she married Eric Linklater, who became a great friend. I stayed with them in Orkney and in Easter Ross. Marjorie is now a great lady in Orkney and our friendship endures to this day.

I spent several week-ends at the Worthing villa, where guests had to be boarded out in neighbouring cottages. Marjorie was usually there too. The old Tiger was invisible all day, but every evening came down to dinner in pyjamas and a macintosh. All the servants were enormous Indians in turbans, and as soon as the old man appeared two of them poured a huge heap of rice on to his plate, to which various delicacies were added. One evening at the end of dinner an Indian handed round long black cigars. I had nervously smoked half of mine when the Indian offered me another. I politely refused it, but the old man growled: 'Take it. You may need it in the night.' Very soon one ceased to be surprised by any eccentricities in this fascinating house. Old Sir Frank Benson was a regular guest – he who had done so much for Shakespeare in the provinces. There was no colour-bar, and I remember John Payne singing operatic arias and Negro spirituals. Another visitor was Paul Robeson: later he had a torrid affair with Yolande, whom he declared was the love of his life.

[6]

At the end of March *The Kinsmen* turned into Sheridan's *School for Scandal*, in which I had the small part of Careless, and was understudy to Eric Portman as Charles Surface. We often had afternoons and evenings off, to make way for the opera company, which in April and May performed *Tannhäuser, Madam Butterfly, Rigoletto, Carmen, Aida, The Magic Flute* and Gounod's *Faust*. Thus I was able to attend a matinée of Ibsen's *Ghosts,* with Mrs Patrick Campbell as Mrs Alving and John

Gielgud as Oswald. The conjunction of two generations was superb, and I can still see and hear Mrs Pat's whispering of 'Ghosts, ghosts'.

On 11 April Eric Portman disappeared with jaundice, and I was called upon to take over his part at next day's matinée. There had been no understudy rehearsals all through the season, and none of us had time to learn parts which we would probably never play. I was lucky, since all Careless's scenes are with Charles Surface, most of whose part I more or less knew. I sat up late learning it all, and next afternoon, when I was standing in the long passage behind the stage, looking at myself in the full-length mirror, to see if my wig and clothes looked all right, Miss Baylis bustled along.

'Do you know your lines, dear boy?'

'I hope so, Miss Baylis.'

'All you've got to do is to be yourself – a perfect gentleman and a bit of a rake (pronounced rike).'

With much help from Ernest, Jean, and John Garside I got through without drying-up. Growing in confidence I played the part again that night, but next day Balliol Holloway, a great favourite at the Vic, took over the part, and I reverted to Careless.

The third week of April was a busy one. On the 21st the company presented *Hamlet* in its entirety, which lasts for five hours. Maurice Farquharson and I played Rosencrantz and Guildenstern, who have a dozen entrances before being shipped off to death in England. I was also Francisco on the battlements in the first scene, later a courtier, a servant, and helped to carry off Hamlet's body. A very exhausting afternoon and evening.

Two days later came the Shakespeare Birthday Festival, which consisted of fifteen scenes from Shakespeare, played by old and new Vic favourites. I played Gratiano in the trial scene of *The Merchant* with Ernest and Edith Evans, also Tranio in a scene from *The Shrew* with Edith Evans and Balliol Holloway. Others involved were John Wyse, Frank Vosper, Ion Swinley and Rupert Harvey. This experienced actor, who boasted that both his grandfathers had been blacksmiths, became a great friend.

Every evening, after the final curtain had fallen, Miss Baylis forced her way through it, wearing the cap and gown of one of her honorary degrees (she was made a Companion of Honour in 1929). All we could hear from behind the curtain, as she addressed the audience, was the many-times-repeated phrase 'thaousand paounds ... thaousand paounds'. She was appealing for contributions to the rebuilding of

Sadlers Wells Theatre, and in the end, aided by great allies such as the
Carnegie Trust and Ninette de Valois, she incredibly got all that was
needed, and in 1931 the theatre reopened under her management, and
the Vic-Wells Ballet was born under Ninette. Meanwhile we students
suffered regular dancing-lessons, usually from one of Ninette's pupils,
but occasionally from the great lady herself. The dancing capacity of
the students was limited.

Two days after the Birthday Festival came the first night of the cut
Hamlet – a difficult job for the cast, who had learned the complete
version and now had desperately to remember where the cuts came.

It was at this time that three new friends came into my life. Two of
them were sisters, Bertha and Irene (always called Rene) Charity. They
came to every Shakespeare performance with two seats in the stalls.
They were always neatly, even smartly dressed. Bertha was crazily in
love with Eric Portman, knowing nothing of his sexual propensities,
and they made friends with him outside the stage-door, and with me
also. Bertha was thirty-three, Rene a pretty little girl of eighteen. They
several times insisted on driving me home to Hans Place in a taxi. I
feebly objected, but Bertha was strong-willed. On my twenty-first
birthday in August they sent me a five-pound note. After the Vic season
I occasionally took them out for the evening, and later Bertha once
visited me in my publishing office. Then I saw them no more; but in 1975
Rene wrote to tell me Bertha had died, and Rene and I corresponded
regularly and happily until her death in 1987.

The third new friend, who was to play an important part in my life,
was James (then known as Jimmy) Hamilton, fresh from a silver
medal for rowing in the Amsterdam Olympics. After an unhappy
apprenticeship with Jonathan Cape he was now running the London
office of the big American publishers Harper, but three years later he
published the first book of Hamish Hamilton Ltd, James becoming
Hamish, and Jimmy Jamie, by which name he was known and loved
thereafter. He came to the Vic courting Jean Forbes-Robertson and
she introduced me to him. They married in 1929 and I was an usher
at their wedding.

The last play of the season was *King Lear* with Ernest and Jean in
great form. I played Burgundy and (heavily disguised) Cornwall's
servant. The opening night was on 14 May, and the next fortnight was
a busy time. On the very next day Deirdre's 'coming out' was celebrated
by a dinner for thirty-six given by Philip Sassoon, followed by a dance
at the Rupert Becketts' in Grosvenor Street. I took Jean to both

entertainments and we giggled a lot at all the grandees, including the Prince of Wales, who stood at the top of the staircase with his watch in his hand, like the White Rabbit, because Mrs Dudley Ward was late. I got to bed at 5 a.m.

Three days later came the much-rehearsed students' matinée performance of Browning's *Pippa Passes*, one of the least unactable of his dramatic works. It tells of a girl silk-weaver who on her only holiday of the year goes singing through the streets of Asolo, near Venice. Her singing as she passes their windows brings to a crisis the lives of four sets of people. I was a young sculptor with a newly-wed Grecian wife. They have apparently been mocked by their friends, but the long speeches are almost impenetrable, and the audience was totally bewildered, though, like all Vic audiences, they clapped us just the same. After all the 'spits and coughs' of recent months it was a joy to declaim in that vast theatre the final lines of our scene:

> Some unsuspected isle in the far seas!
> Like a god going through his world, there stands
> One mountain for a moment in the dusk,
> Whole brotherhoods of cedars on its brow:
> And you are ever by me while I gaze
> – Are in my arms as now – as now – as now!
> Some unsuspected isle in the far seas!
> Some unsuspected isle in far-off seas!

One critic pleased me by writing 'Mr Rupert Hart-Davis has a fine voice and knows how to use it.'

Four days later I took part in a four-handed play by Hubert Henry Davies called *The Mollusc*. Directed by Charlie, this took place in St John's Hall, York Road, in aid of another of Miss Baylis's charities. Gwen Nelson played the main female part with great distinction.

Then Percy Walsh, who was playing the long, important but unrewarding part of Kent in *King Lear*, fell ill, and there was no understudy. Someone remembered that Rupert Harvey had once played the part and he answered the call. He had only a few hours to learn or remember the part, and he very intelligently learned all his cues and all the cues he had to give other people. In between he said what he remembered and otherwise invented bogus and largely meaningless lines in strict Shakespearean metre – an astonishing performance. The audience suspected nothing.

On 1 June the Vic season ended, and I incurred Miss Baylis's displeasure by refusing to appear as a coloured slave in *Aida* in Hud-dersfield for two pounds a week.

[7]

While I was seeking a new job in the theatre I took part in all Deirdre's social activities – dances almost every night, dinner-parties, country-house parties, the Derby, the Fourth of June at Eton, theatres (Pirandello's *Six Characters in Search of an Author*, John Van Druten's dramatisation of Rebecca West's *Return of the Soldier* in which Mary Clare excelled, the Diaghilev Ballet, Paul Robeson singing at Drury Lane) and always bookshops new and secondhand.

In the midst of these diversions I was given a small part in a production of the Stage Society, which had been going since 1899 and had given first performances in England of most of the plays of Shaw, Ibsen and Tchekov. They were a private society and so not bound by the censorship of the Lord Chamberlain. They usually gave one performance on Sunday night and a matinée the next day.

This time they had chosen an interminable play called *Paul among the Jews*, translated from the German of the Austrian poet and novelist Franz Werfel. It lasted for three hours, mostly of talk with little action. St Paul was played by Robert Farquharson, whom William Plomer in another context described as 'a rose-red cissy half as old as time'. There were some splendid old actors in the cast, such as Fewlass Llewellyn, Herbert Lomas and my friend Rupert Harvey. The elder son of the High Priest was played by the dashing young Laurence Olivier. I was the Commander of the Roman troops in Jerusalem in A.D.40. I wrote in my diary: 'All things considered it was amazing that it got through at all. A sticky audience'. The reviews were devastating, one headed 'The Stage Society at its worst', but I enjoyed the whole enterprise, since the Prince of Wales Theatre gave me my first taste of the West End stage. Moreover those two performances brought me the first money I had earned – a cheque for two guineas, signed by Harold Monro and H. F. Rubinstein.

Then, to my delight, Nigel Playfair sent for me and offered me a small part in Goldsmith's *She Stoops to Conquer*, which he was planning to put on in August. I was also to understudy Brian Aherne in the leading rôle of Young Marlow, for four pounds a week. The first rehearsal took place on 16 July and it was delightful to be back in the cosy atmosphere of the Lyric, with most of the same staff, including dear old George Gamble at the stage-door. The first night was a month later, with Hay Petrie as Mr Hardcastle, Marie Ney as Kate, and Playfair himself, fat and fifty-four, as the loutish boy Tony Lumpkin, who according to the text had 'not come to years of discretion yet'. The play ran for nine and a half weeks. I learned all Young Marlow's part by heart, but Brian was obstinately healthy and I had to be contented with the single speech of the drunken servant Jeremy in Act Four.

Playing another small part was Glen Byam Shaw, whom I had seen week after week in J. B. Fagan's weekly repertory company in the tiny Playhouse Theatre at Oxford. We were soon firm friends. One Saturday night I drove him down for the week-end to a house near Bognor which my father had taken for the summer. On the way he suddenly said: 'What do you think of the Baddeley sisters, Angela and Hermione?' I had met them at a country-house party where one evening I acted in charades with them and my friend Nico Llewelyn Davies. Luckily I said: 'I think they're wonderful.' 'Good', said Glen, 'Angela and I have just got engaged.' His question had been wickedly unfair. Later I saw a lot of them, before and after they were married. Now, like me, Glen was an understudy and we attended understudy rehearsals most mornings.

In all the intervals my social life continued, and after a few terrifying driving-lessons in Central London, I acquired my first car – a Morris two-seater, which I greatly enjoyed. On 22 August I wrote in my diary: 'Evening show – came home in the rain, got deliciously wet and suddenly for the first time felt thankful for my luxurious home and comfortable life.'

In the next weeks I saw the end of an old theatrical tradition and the opening of a new one. Fred Terry and his wife Julia Neilson had been playing *The Scarlet Pimpernel* for twenty-five years. They were now much too old for it, and when Fred knelt to kiss Julia's hand he had some difficulty in getting up. But her profile was still beautiful, and they were so identified with their characters that one forgot their age and enjoyed this glimpse of past glory.

In great contrast was the production of the first talking picture in London – Al Jolson in *The Jazz Singer*. The noise, the brashness and Jolson's acting blasted it to success.

Peter Fleming, now in his third year at Oxford, was editor of the undergraduate weekly *Isis* and he asked me to send the paper a regular London Letter for the next two terms. This I did, in the intervals of my other activities. They consisted of short paragraphs about books, music, plays, films, art exhibitions, the motor show and other topical events. I was so pleased with these, my first appearances in print, that I pasted them into a notebook. When I read them again after sixty years I found them touching and amusing.

On 11 October Peter and I attended a packed Albert Hall to hear the famous American 'four-square' gospeller Aimée Semple McPherson. After she had roused the huge audience almost to ecstasy by her exhortations, Peter and I went round to interview her in her dressing-room 'on behalf of Oxford University'. We hadn't prepared any proper questions for this large and impressive lady, so stumblingly asked:

'Don't you find this sort of meeting very tiring?'

'Yes, just look at me. I'm wringing wet all over.'

'Isn't the Albert Hall rather large for such a meeting?'

'No place can be big enough.'

And so it continued. She was charming to us, and by the time we left I felt she thought us 'saved'.

She Stoops to Conquer ended its run on 20 October, to be followed four days later by a double bill of Sheridan's *The Critic* and A. P. Herbert's Shakespearean skit *Two Gentlemen of Soho*. In *The Critic* I had the tiny part of the Master of the Horse and the slightly larger one of the Beefeater. The production was so successful that after four weeks it was transferred for a further five weeks to the Royal Court Theatre in Sloane Square, conveniently near my home in Hans Place.

In November I saw a matinée of Ibsen's *John Gabriel Borkman,* in which Mrs Patrick Campbell and Nancy Price gave superb performances.

Then Deirdre was operated on for appendicitis and I visited her every day in the nursing home and read aloud to her. Hardly a day passed without my buying a new or old book and I read furiously.

During this time I saw a lot of Harman Grisewood, who had started his meteoric B.B.C. career as an uncle in the *Children's Hour* and in time became Controller of the Third Programme, Director of the Spoken Word, and finally Chief Assistant to the Director General. Another visitor was my old Eton friend Jim Lees-Milne, who was being compelled by his father to attend a year's course in shorthand and typing, which he hated. On my free evenings he used to come to Hans Place, where we read and discussed poetry together.

I had a happy reunion with Charlie and his Molly at her family home in Golders Green, and then, through one of Miss Baylis's parsons, got him a wretched job in a boys' camp at Plumstead, near Woolwich. Molly and I visited him there twice.

I saw and loved Jean Forbes-Robertson's first performance as Peter Pan, before *The Critic* closed just in time for me to take train and boat to Monte Carlo, where I saw the New Year in with Deirdre, our cousin Violet and her husband.

1929, which was to prove a year of destiny for me, began with an enjoyable fortnight on the Côte D'Azur and a fraction of Italy, followed by three days in Paris with Deirdre and Marie Ozanne. Back in London I went to a poor play about Byron. When Esmé Percy, a fine actor and well-known homosexual, came down the central staircase during a large party and said 'Nobody has ever been so ravished since Helen of Troy', the audience burst into uncontrollable laughter. Bernard Shaw was visible in the stalls: the only glimpse I ever had of him.

Other plays and excursions culminated in a party at the Lyric, Hammersmith on 27 January, 'to celebrate', as A. P. Herbert put it, 'the Tenth Year of the Benevolent Attempts of SIR NIGEL PLAYFAIR to entertain the Citizens of London'. The evening began with a series of extremely amusing sketches by A.P.H., including skits on all the theatre's successes. The Baddeley sisters performed, along with Edith Evans, Ernest Thesiger, Athene Seyler and many others. Elsa Lanchester and Harold Scott sang, and Arnold Bennett did his best to sing 'Sucking Cider through a Straw'.

After the performance there was dancing on the stage and I saw my friend Leslie Mitchell dancing with a beautiful girl. After the dance I asked him to introduce me to her, and he told me her name was Celia Johnson, and she had a small part in the current play in the theatre, *A Hundred Years Old* by the brothers Quintero. I determined to see her again.

On 3 February I was offered three small parts in a very good anti-war play called *The Rumour* by C. K. Munro at the Royal Court Theatre. Among the large cast were old friends – Maurice Farquharson, John Garside, Rupert Harvey – and a delightful new friend, the director Allan Wade. He had been in the theatre all his life, for some years play-reader for Granville Barker, and he was a great collector of the books of his favourite authors – W. B. Yeats, Conrad, George Moore and Max Beerbohm. He remained a close friend until his death in 1955, and so did his future wife Margot Sieveking, who was also in *The Rumour*. The play opened on 11 February, was well received and ran until 20 April.

Then I at last made contact with Celia Johnson, and for the next

Celia 1929

two months I saw her almost every day, usually driving to fetch her from her home in Richmond and driving her back there after the play at night. I took her to plays and films, the Stage Guild Ball, the Ellen Terry Memorial matinée, to watch the Boat Race from A. P. Herbert's riverside house at Hammersmith, to another Paul Robeson concert at Drury Lane, and for several drives into the country. She had a good sense of humour and we enjoyed the same jokes. I found her ever more attractive, repeatedly told her that I loved her and several times asked her to marry me. All such propositions she brushed aside, and an occasional sisterly peck on the cheek was all my reward. I began to fear that I had no future with her.

Then Nigel Playfair offered me the part of the hero's friend Hastings in a three-week tour of *She Stoops to Conquer* in May. He asked me who I would like to play Miss Neville opposite me. I said 'Celia Johnson, please'. He agreed, but a day or two later telephoned to say that Celia wouldn't do, because in the play Miss Neville and Tony Lumpkin (Playfair himself again) have to stand back-to-back to show that they are the same height, and Celia was considerably taller than Nigel. He told me he had found a good young actress called Peggy Ashcroft, who was just the right height. Pascal said that if Cleopatra's nose had been shorter the whole face of the earth would have changed. If Celia's height had been shorter the whole face of my life would certainly have changed. Such is the power of chance.

Towards the end of March I played a small part in another Sunday night production at the Prince of Wales Theatre. The play, *Hunter's Moon,* adapted from the Danish by Harry Graham, which had been refused a licence by the Lord Chamberlain, took place in the French Revolution. The leading parts were beautifully played by Phyllis Neilson-Terry, Leslie Faber and the young John Gielgud. He was an *emigré* fighting with the Austrians against the revolutionaries, and I was his commanding officer. We both had beautiful white uniforms. In my brief, almost mute and wholly inglorious theatrical career I like to remember that for a moment I trod the boards with Gielgud and Olivier, the two greatest actors of our time, as well as with Dames Sybil Thorndike and Peggy Ashcroft.

On April Fools Day I took Celia to a matinée of Cochran's revue *Wake Up and Dream.* Peter Fleming and his childhood friend Sybil Mayor came with us.

After the end of *The Rumour* I dined on 28 April with my friends Ruth and Tommy Lowinsky at their house in Kensington Square, and had the luck to sit next to Max Beerbohm at dinner, talking to him for most of the meal. Directly I got home I wrote down all I could remember of his sayings. He spoke charmingly of my mother and praised my father's piano-playing. Said that a Paderewski concert made him wish Poland had been crushed. That *Charley's Aunt* had been more of a success in Japan than in China. Plays, he said, should have plenty of action and *no ideas*. He instanced the scene in *The Importance of Being Earnest* where Ernest arrives in full mourning at the gate. The audience are both surprised and prepared. Said he could not abide anything Russian, admitted that the Russians had produced tremendous men, but the hopelessness of their art appalled him. Spoke of Frank Harris as a great talker, quelled only by Oscar Wilde, who Max decided must have been much like Jesus Christ, good-natured and with a Christian spirit. Aubrey Beardsley was the only black-and-white artist worth collecting, because he was the only one whose works were better than their reproductions. He admitted having liked Frank Harris unreservedly in his youth, as moral sense comes only with middle age. Said he could remember everybody's grandfather. Always saying 'me' instead of 'my', and often interpolating 'Don't you know'. An enchanted occasion.

The very next morning I met Peggy Ashcroft at the first rehearsal of the touring company. 'Talked to P.A. Liked her', I wrote in my diary. Two days later, watching her act in a ridiculous play at the Everyman Theatre in Hampstead, I decided she was the best actress I had ever seen, an opinion which the years have only strengthened.

Although the tour was due to open on 13 May I decided to continue rehearsing Galsworthy's three-handed tragedy *The First and the Last*, with Celia and Rupert Harvey, who would also direct. We would give our one performance on the second Sunday of the tour, at the Three Arts Club.

On 7 May I was driving Celia through Grosvenor Square when a car shot out from a side-turning and crashed into us. I was unhurt, but Celia had a sprained ankle, and the car was in a sorry state. For the first week of the tour I hired a Wolseley, whose gears were reluctant to change, and on the morning of 13 May Peg (as I have always called her) and I set out in this unwieldy vehicle for the opening of what was to be for both of us a momentous tour.

[9]

The car caught fire near Bedford, but we managed to reach Cambridge in time to book rooms in a small hotel near the theatre. I shared a dressing-room with Ivan Samson, who played Young Marlow. On Monday the audience was quiet and restrained, but by Wednesday it had become loud and boisterous.

Many of my Eton friends were still undergraduates, and they entertained Peg and me royally. We were together all day, driving to Grantchester, visiting the Fitzwilliam Museum, punting together on the river, alternately reading aloud poems from *The Oxford Book of English Verse*. The Saturday night performance was a riotous success. Playfair made a speech from the stage and the whole company was taken out to supper.

Peg 1929

On Sunday we drove back to London and I rehearsed *The First and the Last* with Celia and Rupert. Next morning I handed back the Wolseley and for £20 hired a pale blue Chrysler for a week. Driving it after the cumbersome Wolseley was like a joy-ride. A picnic lunch on the Downs near Marlborough, and on to Bristol, where we took rooms in the Lyndale Hotel, which was already accommodating the comedians Nervo and Knox and their wives. We had supper with them each night after the play. They were very friendly and extremely funny, and when one of the wives asked me: 'Have you ever played the Grand, Hanley?' I delightedly realised that they accepted us as professionals.

Every day was an excursion – a visit to Cheddar Gorge, bathing at Clevedon, to the suspension bridge by moonlight, a picnic lunch at Glastonbury – and on Friday after the play we drove seventeen miles and climbed Shipham Hill to watch the moon rise over the Mendips. Next day a picnic in Savernake Forest, always reading poetry to each other. The joy-ride was rapidly turning into an idyll.

Back to London on Sunday. The performance of *The First and the Last* seemed to please the audience, in which was Peg. Next morning I sadly surrendered the Chrysler and regained my mended Morris, in which we drove to Oxford and took rooms in the Park End Hotel on

Miss Neville and Hastings, New Theatre, Oxford, May 1927

the way to the station. Here, as at Cambridge, many of my schoolfriends were still undergraduates, and, led by Peter Fleming, they gave our first performance a rapturous reception.

Next day, when Peg had gone on the river with friends, I met in the O.U.D.S. club-room a man who was complaining that his Chrysler was much too big for him and he longed for a smaller car. I told him I had a Morris two-seater outside. We went out to examine the cars, I gave him a cheque for fifty pounds, we exchanged log-books and insurance certificates, and that was that. When Peg came back from the river I said: 'You'll never guess what I've done', and she immediately said 'You've got a Chrysler'. It had been built for the racing motorist Malcolm Campbell, was painted pale yellow, with red leather seats, on which one almost had to lie down to drive. It had a cut-out on the exhaust, which increased its speed and made a most stimulating noise. We were both delighted with it, and after another successful performance of the play 'Talked to Peg till 3 a.m. We love each other.'

Next morning we breakfasted with the Playfairs in the Trout at Godstow. Afterwards we sat in a field reading poetry and deciding to get married as soon as possible. Then we attended a lunch given by the O.U.D.S. to the whole company. Thursday and Friday I described in my diary as 'lovelier than anything I have ever known'.

But there was a snag. Before the beginning of the tour I had promised Celia that on the final Saturday I would drive to Richmond early in the morning and take her to Oxford for the matinée. I felt that I couldn't disappoint her, so I duly fetched her and on the way back, as we were driving through Maidenhead Thicket, I told her I was going to marry Peg. She immediately burst into hysterical tears, sobbing that she had always loved me. I said it was a pity she had never even suggested such a thing before, and now, alas, it was too late.

She was still very distressed when we got to Oxford, and there was some time to fill before the matinée. Luckily I saw Peter walking down the street. I hailed him, told him Celia was very unhappy and asked him to get her something to eat and drink, take her to the theatre, fetch her after the play and take her to the station to catch a London train. All of which, bless him, he obediently did.

And so, after a rousing last performance and a long talk with Peg, my acting career came to an end.

INTERLUDE : AT HOME AND ABROAD

> Travel, in the younger sort, is a part of education;
> in the elder, a part of experience.
>
> BACON

[1]

I FELT very sad about Celia, and slightly guilty. In an attempt to soften the blow I once again took her to plays and films and drove her about. My uncle Duff Cooper and his wife Diana had been wonderfully good to me since my mother's death, asking me to lunch or dinner to meet their literary friends – Maurice Baring, Hilaire Belloc, J.M. Barrie and others. Now they asked me to stay at their house on the Sussex coast near Bognor. It was a happy place, of sunshine, bathing, Duff reading aloud, friends coming and going. One day Diana said: 'Rupert is just like his Uncle Duff. Put him in a comfortable chair with a good book and he's no trouble.'

The highspot of my visit was the arrival of Belloc for dinner. One of his poems ended:

> The passer-by shall hear me still,
> A boy that sings on Duncton Hill.

And I remembered these lines when he arrived late for dinner because his car had broken down on Duncton Hill. As ever, he was dressed in scruffy black clothes, cloak and hat. As he approached the company on the lawn he cried out: 'I am thirsty, my children, I must have beer.' Duff always kept a copious cellar, but beer was not one of his drinks, and some had to be sent for.

Dinner was out of doors on a lovely June evening. Belloc ate voraciously and talked amusingly, as glasses of beer, sherry, white wine, claret, port and brandy gradually piled up beside him. Suddenly he noticed them, exclaiming: 'God damn my soul to hell, I must drink this up,' and downed them in quick succession in the right order. Then he effortlessly continued his flow of talk, saying: 'Baths, making love, and wine corrupt the body – and life consists of wine, making love and baths.' Said he wrote his life of James II at Biskra in the desert – 'forty-seven mistakes, including howlers'. Talked a lot about prose and rhetoric, never called his own poems anything but 'my verses'. Said 'Nothing matters but the salvation of the soul, and the terrible bore is that no one knows what it is.' Wished he had writen *one* thing to be remembered by – like Young's *Night Thoughts* – a curious choice. Then he sang some of his songs in a high tenor voice. A delightful man.

Other visitors included Maurice Baring, A.E.W. Mason and my mother's old lover Sidney Herbert.

Then, on 24 June, I took Celia to a play, drove her home to Richmond and 'more or less said goodbye. Very very sad and hating myself like hell. Poor darling.' Soon afterwards Peg came back to London. We drove into the country and visited her guardians, a little martinet of a retired brigadier and his delightful wife. Peg's father had been killed in the war and her mother had died in 1926. It was from her that Peg inherited her love of poetry and drama. Now we drove to South Harting, in Surrey, one of her favourite places. Next day a picnic on Merrow Down, where we read Kipling's poems aloud.

I had long arranged to go with Peter Fleming on a driving holiday through France and Spain to Corsica. The day before we started Peg and I bought identical loose-leaf notebooks, in which we wrote daily letters to each other, posting the relevant leaves to be inserted in the other book. The one containing my letters has survived, Peg's has not.

[2]

We drove off from Hans Place in Peter's open Morris two-seater in the early morning of 17 July, carrying with us two small tents and other camping equipment. My travelling library consisted of *The Forsyte Saga*, three Hardy novels, *Vanity Fair, Lavengro, The Path to Rome*, Bacon's Essays and several books of poetry, all of which I read and enjoyed. We crossed from Dover to Calais in a cargo-boat with ten other passengers. One of them, wearing dirty green shorts and a hairnet, Peter decided must be a Swiss naval attaché. No Customs or passport. We soon flashed past a notice saying GOUDRON FRAIS, swung round a corner and were instantly sprayed with red-hot liquid tar. By the time we got to Versailles we were so tired and dirty that we decided

Departure from
Hans Place

camping should begin tomorrow. The AA Book said that the best hotel was the Trianon Palace, one of the grandest and most expensive in France. However we got a large room with two comfortable beds and its own bathroom at two pounds for the night.

Next day we lunched at Chartres, admired the cathedral and drove on to camp near the battlefield of Poitiers. Most of the next day was spent in a heat-wave at Bordeaux, taking hours to cash travellers' cheques and obtain Spanish visas from the British Consul. Driving on, we at last reached the Atlantic coast at a little holiday resort called Mimizan Plage. We had hardly sighted the sea before the car stuck more than axle-deep in sand. A jovial bunch of holiday-makers contrived to free us with spades, planks and sacks, and we gratefully leaped into the sea ('one of the most enjoyable things I have ever done'). We slept in the dunes, without tents but with plenty of mosquitoes, and at dawn we suddenly saw a rainbow over the sea. Just time to dash in and out of the water before a torrent of rain fell on us. Through it we drove to Bayonne, Biarritz, St Jean de Luz, Hendaye, and so into Spain. We slept in a Bilbao hotel, and decided that we would abandon our plan of driving as far as Corunna, so at Santander we turned back and drove south-east through Vittoria and Pamplona to the lovely St Jean-Pied-de-Port under the pass of Roncevaux, where we crossed into France and had an excellent dinner and sleep at an inn by a waterfall.

When we reached Pau we bought a copy of *The Times* and learned that Peter had got a First in English. At Carcassonne the car collapsed and we had to wait for eighteen hours while it was mended. Then on through Avignon and Aix-en-Provence to Cannes.

There we discovered that Peter had somehow lost four hundred francs, leaving us almost penniless. I suddenly remembered my last happy summer holiday with my mother three years ago at the Hôtel du Roc at Antibes. I was sure we would find someone there to vouch for us.

Sure enough in a grand new glass-fronted restaurant on the cliff-top I spotted an Eton friend Phil Kindersley, lunching with his wife Oonagh Guinness, the actress June and her protector Lord Inverclyde, whose yacht was anchored off-shore. They were all dressed in the smartest yachting clothes. I was in filthy shirt and shorts, grimy and unshaved. Phil was obviously appalled by this apparition and quickly agreed to sponsor the cheque which Peter had made out. Lord Inverclyde was more friendly and stood me a double brandy. Thus, once again solvent, we drove on to Nice, where at the waterfront we met Peter's widowed mother and his brother Ian.

At noon on 28 July we all four embarked for Corsica on the *Emperor Bonaparte*. Darkness was falling when we reached Bastia on the north-east coast of the island. The ship could not be got alongside the jetty until some men swam out with ropes. Even then each piece of luggage had to be let down on a cord, loaded on to a donkey-cart and thrashed up a slope to the car and chauffeur which Peter had somehow managed to charter. The drive of sixty miles across the island to Algajola took three hours, since the road was little more than a mule-track, pitted with crevasses and dotted with boulders. The driver, a jovial man, was clearly something of a hunter, for whenever our headlights picked out an animal near the road he cried out '*Un lapin, holà*' and pursued it across country and between trees. None was caught.

When we reached the outskirts of Algajola the whole place was in darkness. On the road we met a young man dressed like a poet, with a cloak and broad-brimmed hat. When the driver asked him the way to the Castle Inn, he began: '*Au fond du village vous trouverez un monument aux morts.*' To which the driver wittily replied: '*Cela ne m'étonne pas*'. The young man walked off in a huff, but we somehow found the house, could wake nobody, forced an entry, went downstairs in search of food, when suddenly all the lights fused. Luckily I had my torch, so we seized some bottles of Evian water, stumbled upstairs, found ourselves empty bedrooms and sank into bed utterly exhausted.

The house turned out to be a lovely place, an old fortress, the *modern* part built in 1560 on Roman remains. Apart from some twenty cottages there was nothing to be seen but mountains behind and the bluest sea in front, with a sandy beach alongside. We bathed five or six times a day, then lay in the hot sun and read our books. Ian had brought a gramophone, on which he played a number of sentimental songs. The food was good, and the mosquito-nets effective. There were three tame hares on the terrace in front of the house.

Our first day there was, I knew, to be the first night in Blackpool of the pre-London tour of Ashley Dukes's adaptation of Lion Feuchtwanger's long novel *Jew Süss*, in which Peg later had her first West End success. I felt ridiculously nervous as evening approached. My letters to Peg during this whole trip are full of love and longing, intermixed with an account of all our doings.

It was an idyllic place for a holiday, but the Fleming boys soon became restless. Ian discovered a brace of *louche* homosexuals living in the hills and spent a lot of time playing cut-throat bridge with them. Peter went on an abortive boar-hunt with the local mayor, but left us on 4 August to drive non-stop from Nice to Perthshire for the start of the grouse-shooting. We were delighted to find that the butcher and baker in neaby Ile-Rousse were called Casanova and Casabianca. Ian and his mother argued a good deal, but we were cheered by the arrival of a German couple, the husband a criminal lawyer. He despised the Corsicans, whom he described as '*anspruchlos und hundert Jahre zurück*'.

On the night of 11 August we embarked on a boat for Nice. Ian and I were put with a Corsican in a stifling cabin in the bowels of the ship, Mrs Fleming in one with three battered females. Ian lay down and went to sleep in our cabin, but his mother and I thought we'd rather sit on deck. We had just hired chairs and pillows when I spotted two doors marked *Cabine de Luxe*. They proved to be empty, so we took one each for forty francs and slept very well.

At Nice Ian drove off to Austria, leaving me to conduct his mother to London. She had a great deal of luggage, large and small, the most tiresome piece of it an elaborate and heavy tea-basket for one, containing a spirit-lamp, a kettle, a teapot, one cup, one saucer and one plate. It was awkward to carry.

I took a third-class ticket to London, which cost the equivalent of £3.10. Mrs Fleming travelled first-class. At 6 p.m. she came along to tell me that the train wasn't due in Paris till 5 a.m., so we decided to disembark at Lyon and stay the night there. At the Carlton Hotel Mrs F was delighted when we were taken for a honeymoon couple and offered a double-bedded room. We preferred two single ones. Next day was all train, followed by a night at the very cheap Hôtel Chevreuse in Paris. Then after three weary days of travelling we reached London. When I had safely deposited Mrs F in a taxi with all her luggage she graciously presented me with the tea-basket, as a reward for 'being so good with Ian'.

[3]

Before I left for my continental trip I decided that I would never be more than a mediocre actor (my height of six foot three didn't help) and sternly told Peg that one of us should have a fixed income. I had always had a passion for books and reading, so publishing seemed a good idea. Jimmy Hamilton was the only publisher I knew, and I asked him if he could find me a job in the business. He promised to do his best, and when I got home from Corsica I found a letter from him saying that Charley Evans, the head of Heinemann's, was looking for a young man, and he had arranged for me to lunch with them both in two days' time.

Next day he telephoned to say that Charley had just published a new author's first novel, of which he had great hopes, and it would be helpful if I mentioned it during our lunch. I dashed round to the Times Book Club and obtained a copy of the book, which I read straight through with pleasure until 2 a.m. It was called *The Man Within* by Graham Greene.

Our lunch at the Garrick Club passed off well, and it may have been my flattering reference to the book which prompted Charley to offer me an unspecified job at two pounds a week for the first year, four pounds for the second, and then whatever he thought I was worth. A fixed income at last! Peg was already earning fifteen pounds a week. I learned later that Charley had interviewed other applicants, and I owed his choice of me entirely to the good offices of Jimmy. I was to report for duty at the end of September.

I had stupidly agreed, some time before, to appear in an amateur production of Rostand's three-handed play *Les Deux Pigeons* with Denys Buckley and a French girl called Ginette Spanier, who later, after a terrible time in occupied France, became an arbiter of fashion as directress of the House of Balmain. We rehearsed in her parents' house in Golders Green, and before we left she asked us to sign her visitors' book. It had this printed heading:

DATE	NAME	ARRIVAL	DEPARTURE

I wrote

17th Aug	Rupert Hart-Davis	debonair	hurried

which they (and I) thought rather amusing. We gave two performances, which seemed quite successful, at a fête in the garden of Denys's family home in Sussex, but I swore an oath never again to appear as an amateur actor, and I never have.

Meanwhile *Jew Süss* was on its triumphant way through the cities of the north, and Peg's and my daily letters always arrived next morning. Those were the days.

On 23 August I drove in the yellow Chrysler (which we had christened Emily) to Norfolk to spend the week-end with my dear friend Wyndham Ketton-Cremer and his parents in their lovely seventeenth-century house Felbrigg, near Cromer. Next day Wyndham had to go out in the afternoon and I had tea with his father and an old friend, Mr H., whom I described to Peg:

'He is a Norwich solicitor of about sixty-five. He cares for and speaks of nothing but Norfolk, of which he has a prodigious if indiscriminate knowledge. His moustache is as big and bushy as it could possibly be, and yet his eyebrows are bigger and bushier. He is a confirmed

Emily, the Chrysler

bachelor and drinks port sacramentally. At tea the talk was of Norfolk cricket, partridges and rainfall. Apparently the year 1879, which they both remember vividly, was phenomenally productive of both birds and water.'

From Felbrigg I drove to Glasgow, to spend my twenty-second birthday with Peg in the house of her delightful Scottish Uncle Jim and Auntie Flo. On the way I gave a lift to an old woman who tried to give me a vegetable marrow in gratitude. I was delighted and excited by *Jew Süss*, in which Peg and Matheson Lang led a most distinguished cast. The play was set in eighteenth-century Germany, the incidental music (mostly Scarlatti) was conducted by Constant Lambert, and the ballet was by Marie Rambert, choreographed by Frederick Ashton.

Next day I sped southward to be an usher on 31 August at the wedding of Jimmy and Jean. I had received instructions from the head usher, Sammy Edgar. They ended: 'A small ferrety-looking person at the door will be me'. This indication was apt, since all the other ushers were gigantic rowing blues or Olympic oarsmen. Our orders were strict: holders of cards with crosses on them in one part of the church; cards without crosses in another; anyone without a card to be thrown out. But nobody had told us that *two* of the invited guests were deaf-and-dumb. Luckily one of them was Donald Gollan, who had won the Diamond Sculls at Henley and was known to all, but the other poor wretch was a distant relation of the Forbes-Robertsons, who arrived looking furtive in a pink shirt. On being asked to produce his card he could only squeak and grunt, so was speedily frog-marched by two huge blues to a remote part of the organ-loft.

In a joint letter from their honeymoon Jean wrote: 'At the reception we had some pretty queer "wedding remarks". Miss Baylis's was "As I was on me knees, saying me prayers to God, dear child, I couldn't help taking a peep at your dear father. He looked so beautiful, and I felt sure God wouldn't mind."'

A day or two later I drove to Winchelsea, where Rupert Harvey and his family were holidaying in a hut on the beach. I stayed for two days, sleeping in a small tent and spending most of the daytime reading my future employers' latest winner, *The Good Companions*. From there I drove to Bath to stay a couple of nights with my beloved Aunt Madge, and then drove non-stop to Birmingham for the last week of the tour. Emily, the yellow Chrysler, was now consuming as much oil as water, and a great deal of both: also her brake-drums were said to need repairing. Sadly I decided that if I got her safely back to London I would sell her.

The Birmingham week was pure enjoyment, staying in the same hotel as Peg, watching the play every night, and getting to know some of the rest of the company. Two of them became lifelong friends. One was Veronica Turleigh, whom I had seen week after week in the Playhouse Theatre at Oxford: she was now married to James Laver, author and museum curator. The other was that fine actor Felix Aylmer, whose two interesting books, *Dickens Incognito* and *The Drood Case*, I published more than thirty years later. Marie Rambert and her husband Ashley Dukes were also there, and one day we picnicked with them by the river at Stratford-on-Avon. At the end of the week we drove safely to London.

Jew Süss opened at the Duke of York's Theatre on 19 September. Crowds had been queueing for thirty hours to secure places in pit and gallery. The house was packed, the applause tumultuous. Next day the critics were unanimous in their praise of the play, Lang and Peg. In *The Times* Charles Morgan wrote: 'We should need to be blind to miss the distinction of Miss Peggy Ashcroft's performance, which, though of no great substance, did give integrity to one character and did communicate an emotion not directly of theatrical origin,' and St John Ervine in the *Observer*: 'Perhaps the most attractive performance of all was that of Miss Peggy Ashcroft, a young actress of whom I had not before heard. She acted with a proud innocence that was exquisitely lovely.' Desmond MacCarthy tore the play to pieces at some length in the *New Statesman*, but clearly it was set for a long run.

I spent most evenings at the theatre in front, and behind the scenes, where I made several new friends. One was a Cambridge undergraduate who had acquired a back-stage job in the vacation. When Peg had to commit suicide by throwing herself out of a window it was he who caught her. His name was Alistair Cooke.

Another delightful friend was an elderly Jewish actor called Doré Lewin Mannering. In his youth he had accidentally killed a young colleague in a stage-fight and was ever afterwards haunted by this horror. He formed a huge collection of books on folk-lore and anthropology, but when he reached ten thousand volumes he thought that was enough and sold the lot. By the time we knew him he had begun to miss the books so much that he started collecting again, and found himself buying back many of his old favourites. For a wedding present he gave us a copy of *The Opera Book* by Edith B. Ordway, which gives the plots of all the classic operas and has been a great help to me down the years.

And then, on the last day of September, I drove down to Surrey to begin my publishing career.

PART TWO : THE BOOK-TRADE

*C'est un métier que de faire un
livre comme de faire une
pendule; il faut plus que de
l'esprit pour être auteur.*
JEAN DE LA BRUYÈRE

[1]

WILLIAM HEINEMANN came of a German-Jewish family which had
been naturalised English by his father in 1856. He was educated in
Dresden and England and was fluent in French, German and Italian.
He served his publishing apprenticeship with the firm of Trübner and
started his own business in 1890. Realising that he needed a stalwart
English partner he made an excellent choice in Sydney Pawling, a tall
cricketing Englishman popular with everyone, who was on the staff of
Mudie's Library and an expert in the commercial side of book-selling.
The partnership worked admirably. The firm's first book was *The
Bondman* by Hall Caine, which had a huge sale, and was quickly followed
by Whistler's *Gentle Art of Making Enemies*. Thereafter Heinemann
specialised in foreign literature, commissioning Constance Garnett to
translate Dostoevsky, Turgenev, and Tolstoy, and publishing the Loeb
Classical Library of translations of the Greek and Latin classics, but
his list of English authors was impressive – Beerbohm, Masefield,
Galsworthy, Conrad, George Moore, Maugham, H. G. Wells.

Heinemann died in 1920 aged fifty-seven. After his death Fryn
Tennyson Jesse wrote: 'He was a man to whom the dream was more
than the business,' and Masefield: 'He made publishing a fastidious,
discriminating work of art, and built up his list like an architect.'

Soon after his death the business was bought by the American
publisher F. N. Doubleday, known in the firm by the acronym of his
initials Effendi. One of his first actions was to order the building of a

huge edifice near Kingswood in Surrey, the counterpart to his large
Garden City Press on Long Island. It was a U-shaped building with
a grass lawn in the middle. The printing and binding departments
were on the ground floor, boardroom and offices above. It was called
the Windmill Press, after the colophon of a windmill which William
Nicholson had drawn for Heinemann and was now printed on the title-
page of most of the firm's books.

[2]

I reported somewhat nervously to the Editorial Department, which
in one room already housed four men, busily reading manuscripts, and
a superb secretary called Grace Cranston. The most interesting of the
inhabitants was a little gnome-like man called Arnold Haskell, who
later became a famous balletomane, writer on the ballet and Director
of the Royal Ballet School. It was common knowledge that his wealthy
father had promised him a large allowance on condition that he
obtained a salaried job. He read faster than anyone I have known,
getting through twice as many manuscripts as anyone else, and wrote
succinct, often witty, reports. In his spare time he was working on one
of the earliest of his many books, a series of interviews with Jacob
Epstein, which appeared in 1932 as *The Sculptor Speaks*.

After a few days he kindly offered to drive me down from London
and back each day in his Austin Seven. I gratefully accepted his offer,
only to find that he was in the earliest stage of being taught to drive
by his father's chauffeur. Those journeys were terrifying, but I thought
it would be unkind to revert to my own car. By the time my stint at
Kingswood was over he was almost in control of the vehicle, though
the faithful chauffeur was still at his side.

The oldest of the readers was Arnold Gyde, a most accomplished
editor: he had been wounded in the war, and was married to a singer
who had just presented him with his first child, to whom he spent some
time each day cooing on the office telephone. The others were Warren
Zambra, who had translated the Kaiser's *Memoirs* into English, and
Paul Weston Edwards, whose job it was to dish out manuscripts (the
firm was deluged with them) to the rest of us according to subject. My
ration consisted of novels, most of them hopelessly incompetent and
unpublishable.

One day Paul called out: 'Can any of you stand Mary Webb?' I said:
'Yes, I can,' and he passed me an extremely long typescript, which he

thought resembled Mary Webb. I read it conscientiously and wrote a report strongly recommending it for publication. My opinion was upheld by the firm's official reader, Frank Swinnerton, who many years later became a close friend, and the book appeared in 1931, *The Shiny Night* by Beatrice Tunstall. It was the first of innumerable books for which I was to be responsible, and when I first re-read it sixty years later I was happy to find that my instinct had been right.

[3]

Soon after this Peg and I visited the Lavers in their top-floor flat in Piccadilly, and when they told us they were moving at the end of the year we were sure it was just the place for us, and we managed to obtain a lease at £160 a year. This decided us to get married during the theatre's three-day Christmas break and to move into the flat in January.

We were married on Monday, 23 December (the day after Peg's twenty-second birthday) in St Saviour's, Walton Place, behind Hans Place. Only our closest family were there, and Harman Grisewood was my best man. After we had knelt for the parson's blessing, the only thing Peg's guardian said to us was 'You both need your shoes mending'. Nothing daunted we crawled into Arnold Haskell's Austin Seven, which he had kindly lent us, and drove away. Our first night we spent at the Oxford hotel where we had plighted our troth, our second at an inn at Painswick in the Cotswolds, and on our way back to London we visited William Nicholson and his family at Sutton Veny in Wiltshire. So ended the fateful year of 1929.

[4]

Early in January 1930 we moved into the flat at 213 Piccadilly. It contained a large sitting-cum-dining room stretching the whole width of the building and looking across to Swan & Edgar's on the edge of the Circus. At night in this room one could see to read by the light of the advertisements outside. At the back there was a small bedroom, a largish bathroom and a tiny kitchen and hall. Since I had been collecting books from my schooldays I already had a considerable number. I hired an old man to carry them up the four flights of stairs, a sackful at a time. When the last sack had been hauled up he took off his cap,

The Young Marrieds

mopped his brow and said: 'Coo, it wouldn't 'alf make your 'ead ache to read this lot'.

Our first visitors, on 11 January, were my sister Deirdre and her future husband Ronnie Balfour, Harman Grisewood and William Nicholson, all of whom signed the slim visitors' book, in which all who later made the steep ascent were persuaded to follow suit. If one wants to drop names it is better to do it in a cloud-burst rather than in odd spots, and to avoid cluttering up this narrative I have relegated part of the cloud-burst to Appendix A on p. 182.

On the floor below us, the third, there was a flat just like ours. Below that there were four separate rooms, occupied by ladies of the night, to judge by the empty stout-bottles and other objects outside on the landing every morning. One of the rooms was rented by a professional co-respondent who had been hired by a friend of my father's to provide evidence for his divorce. Below them were a house-agent's office and a hairdressing saloon, which we suspected was a white-slave centre, because of the huge baskets which kept coming and going. On the ground-floor there was only a passage leading to the stairs.

Later, when I was working in London, the hairdresser hired an old man to walk up and down outside with a sandwich-board saying 'WHOLE HEAD 21/-'. One day when I came home to lunch I learned that the co-respondent had returned from an engagement with a lot of luggage, which the old man, taking off his sandwich-board, kindly offered to carry up for her. Half-way along the passage he fell down dead, and when I arrived the body was still on the floor, and the co-respondent was in the arms of the *soi-disant* hairdresser, sobbing and crying: 'I've killed him. I've killed him.' There was certainly plenty of activity in the building.

On 24 April Deirdre and Ronnie were married in Westminster Cathedral. Deirdre was a Roman Catholic, but Ronnie was not, so it was a mixed marriage, mercifully shorter than the full nuptial mass. As an usher I conducted hordes of people up what must be the longest aisle in Christendom. They spent their honeymoon at Portofino, and then settled into 24 Wellington Square, Chelsea, which remained in the family for many years.

Deirdre's Wedding

[5]

Jew Süss closed in March after more than two hundred performances, and almost immediately Peg was engaged to play Desdemona to Paul Robeson's Othello. This production should have been a masterpiece, for Robeson had a fine presence, a magnificent voice and a perfect ear, so that he could reproduce any intonation given to him, but none such was available. The play was presented by Maurice Browne, an Englishman who had spent most of his acting life in America. He cast himself for Iago, a difficult part far beyond his grasp, and worst of all hired his American ex-wife Ellen Van Volkenburg as director. She spent most of the rehearsals in the front row of the dress-circle, with a rose in one hand and a megaphone in the other. Robeson badly needed direction: he had no experience of speaking Shakespearean blank verse, or of wearing Elizabethan costume, which didn't suit him, until the last act, when he looked superb in a full-length white robe, but in none of these difficulties did he receive any help or coaching.

One week-end we travelled down to Dartington Hall, near Totnes in Devon, where Leonard Elmhirst and his wealthy American wife were in process of starting their famous – later infamous – school. Presumably they were helping to finance *Othello*.

On the morning after our arrival Peg, Paul and I went for a walk after breakfast, and when we returned we found on the hall-table a roneoed sheet, on which the first two items were

(1) Mr and Mrs Hart-Davis and Mr Paul Robeson have arrived and will leave on Monday.

(2) The recuperative power of the soya bean is now established.

This juxtaposition made us laugh immoderately and Paul rolled on the floor with tears pouring down his cheeks. The vision of this gigantic Negro helpless with laughter on the floor of the great fourteenth-century hall will remain with me always.

While they rehearsed I happily read the novels of Peacock in the garden. Next morning at breakfast Miss Van Volkenburg said to me: 'You see, Mr Hart-Davis, the trouble is that Act 3 Scene 3 slopes so.' I commiserated with her on this pretentious and idiotic remark.

Back in London the play opened at the Savoy Theatre on 19 May. The scenery had been designed by the old artist James Pryde, and as in so many of his paintings the final scene contained a four-poster bed fourteen foot high. Miss Van Volkenburg had been so insufferably rude to Pryde that he took his revenge by making much of the movable

Peg as Desdemona

scenery of cement rather than papier mâché, so that every scene-change made the front-cloth scenes almost inaudible, owing to the noise of winches shifting the weighty masses. One evening I ran into Pryde behind the dress-circle and as the intolerable noise continued he chuckled 'There's several hundredweight in that lot'.

Despite all these handicaps, the steadying performances of Sybil Thorndike's Emilia and young Ralph Richardson's Roderigo enabled the power of Paul's personality to break through, and when he cried out: 'I would have him *nine years* a-killing' you could hear the audience draw in its breath in terror. The critics damned the production, but

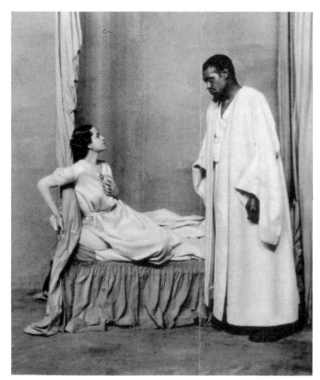

'*Have you prayed
tonight, Desdemona?*'

praised Paul's performance lavishly, and Peg's Desdemona was universally acclaimed. The play ran for six weeks and I watched it at least
a dozen times, so that I came to know it almost as well as those seven
Shakespeare plays at the Vic.

We saw a lot of Paul off stage and both became very fond of him.
He was gentle, modest, affectionate and full of fun. He was one of the
only four people who always called me Rupe. The others were William
Nicholson, Ian Fleming and Jamie Hamilton – a diverse but distinguished quartet. One day when I teased him by calling him a great
black brute, he said: 'Garn, it's only sunburn'. He took us to see and
hear Chaliapin in *Boris Godunov*, and never, before or since, have I been
so impressed and carried away by any performer. His voice and his
physical presence were almost overpowering.

[6]

Ever since I left the Vic I had kept in touch with Charlie Marford by letters. His were as racy as his conversation, and came from all over the place – Saltburn-by-the-Sea in Yorkshire, Rochdale in Lancashire, Newport in Monmouthshire, Tonypandy in Wales. This last recalled an incident when he was touring with Ben Greet's Shakespeare company, performing to schools. During a performance of *The Merchant of Venice* before a large audience of girls, Charlie, playing one of his usual 'spits and coughs', was waiting in the wings for his brief entrance in the trial scene. Beside him was a stage-hand who, Charlie learned in a whispered conversation, came from Tonypandy, which Charlie knew. He suddenly realised that he had missed his cue, rushed on to the stage and said:

> 'My lord, here stays without
>   A messenger with letters from the doctor,
>   New come from Tonypandy.'
> *Greet* (playing the Duke): 'From *where*, Marford?'
> *Charlie*: 'From Padua, sir'.
> *Greet*: 'That's not what you said the first time, Marford'.
> *Charlie*: 'No, sir'.
> *Greet*: 'What did you say the first time, Marford?'
> *Charlie*: 'Tonypandy, sir'.
> *Greet*: 'There's no such place in Shakespeare, Marford.'
> *Charlie*: 'No, sir.'

Then the Duke carried on with the trial, and the girls took this interlude in their stride.

Now he was back in Tonypandy, with Molly at his side, where she remained for the rest of his life, though his wife refused to divorce him. They played in provincial repertory companies, one-night stands in village halls, tours that soon collapsed. They earned very little, but each week, without fail, they sent at least two pounds to Charlie's family.

Then in 1929 they spent the best part of a year in Ireland, which Charlie always loved. They underwent a lengthy and wide-ranging tour of remote towns and villages throughout the republic. One of Charlie's letters is headed:

> Edenderry today
> God knows where tomorrow.

They were both part of the Irish actor-manager Anew McMaster's Shakespeare company. Charlie was playing 'seconds' – Macduff, the King in *Hamlet* and so on – while Molly had successes as Ophelia and Desdemona. Charlie reported:

> We are trapesing round the smallest dates you could possibly imagine, two-or-three-night stands and very wild Western, believe me. How we ever get on the stages (save the mark) is a marvel. We journey twice a week and never do fewer than nine shows, including matinées and every Sunday. We're rehearsing *Stoops*. I play Tony Lumpkin. Molly's right out of this, so she'll be able to go round and start the applause for me, ditto laughs.

After the tour Charlie attempted to run a repertory theatre and his first letter from there is headed:

Civic Theatre

Dun Laoghaire

(What a stupid way to spell Dunleary).

For the first play they rehearsed *Blackmail*, 'but the priests walked in and banned the play. Consternation. To cut a long story short, in desperation, we put on *Macbeth*. It was the only thing we COULD do at all. The Macbeth has only just become an actor (pro). He had played the part somewhere with amateurs, a very cut version, and he HAD to do it for us. I played Macduff. Banquo's lines in the dark scene were spoken by me in a huddle of figures grouped down stage, and I definitely went on and depicted Duncan, First Murderer, and the Doctor. After the first scene, when Banquo got disentangled from the group, he had to speak his own essential lines, but you'd be amazed at the number of things he is credited with in the book that are said by other people in our version. Next week we play *Oliver Twist*. I am Fagin. Surely they won't ban THAT?'

After another week or two the whole enterprise collapsed through lack of money. Charlie and Molly did some variety acts in village halls round Dublin, and then this Irish venture was over.

[7]

Back to Peg and me. After *Othello* came Somerset Maugham's new play *The Breadwinner*, with Ronald Squire and Marie Löhr in the chief parts, Peg and Jack Hawkins as their children. Before the London opening there was a try-out at Eastbourne, for the first night of which Maugham booked the six front rows of stalls and invited some of his grand London friends to attend the performance and a lavish supper at the Grand Hotel, where they would all be put up for the night at his expense.

After the performance, which had gone well, we were leaving the theatre by the stage-door with Maugham when we heard loud female sobbing from one of the dressing-rooms. We discovered that it came from the other girl in the play, who had been extremely nervous, since this was her first important rôle, and had fluffed some of her lines. She was being roundly ticked off by the director, a stupid and insensitive man. Maugham sent him on to the hotel and sat with the girl till she recovered and dressed. She told him her fiancé had bicycled half across England to see the play and was waiting outside. When she was ready Maugham took them both to the hotel and sat them on each side of him at the supper. When, years later in his daughter's house, I reminded him of this very touching incident, he denied any recollection of it. He was by nature a sentimentalist who managed, most of the time, to conceal his true feelings under a blanket of worldly cynicism. The play opened at the Vaudeville Theatre in London on 30 September. It received mixed reviews but ran for 158 performances.

[8]

I had now been happily transferred from Kingswood to Heinemann's London headquarters, a stately Queen Anne house in Great Russell Street. The hall, which was furnished by a glass box containing the receptionist and telephone operator, gave birth to a wide semi-circular staircase leading to the first floor. At the end of the hall was a large waiting-room, in the far corners of which were two tiny rooms. One had been turned into a lavatory, the other was my place of work. There was just room in it for a substantial desk and a chair on each side of it. The second one was used by the firm's delightful London traveller, Roger Hutchinson, who was there only in the evening when he wrote out his day's orders.

My main duties were to act as factotum to the Managing Director Charley Evans. He had been a schoolmaster, Educational Editor of Edward Arnold Ltd, and from 1914 to 1921 General Manager of Heinemann's. After Heinemann's death he became Managing Director.

He was a small, balding, undistinguished-looking man of forty-eight with a great flair for literary merit. For instance he spotted the promise in Margaret Kennedy's first, rather ordinary, novel, and her next was *The Constant Nymph*, a runaway success. Even as Heinemann had chosen Pawling to grace his board, so did Evans choose a large, amiable, imposing-looking man called Theodore Byard (though his real name was thought to be Sprat). He had a vague reputation as a concert singer, but knew little of books and nothing of publishing. He caused stifled mirth at editorial meetings, particularly when he insisted on calling *Into the Abyss* by John Knittel *Into the Abbess*.

The board was completed when Doubleday, without consulting Evans, appointed a journalist called A. S. Frere-Reeves (he later dropped the Reeves) a director of the firm. Evans bitterly resented this, and the relationship of the two men was at best an armed neutrality, so that the office was not a very happy place.

Evans was not an easy man to work for, and if I succeeded in doing something on his behalf which he thought he should have done himself he accused me of 'stealing his thunder' – a preposterous accusation to a two-pounds-a-week dogsbody from the Managing Director. My duties were varied – some editorial work and proof-reading, running errands for Evans, and interviewing in the waiting-room writers and others whom the directors were unwilling or too busy to see. One day George Moore, aged seventy-nine and very tottery, was waiting to see Evans, when an exuberant and loud-speaking man selling disinfectants for telephone-receivers was let loose on me. 'We have examined a thousand London mouthpieces, analysed their contents and discovered x per cent of this germ, y per cent of that poison, etc etc, and finally we discovered *ten per cent* of *horse-manure!*' Although Moore always refused to have a telephone in his house, he was terrified of germs and illness, and by the time I got rid of the salesman the old writer was on the edge of collapse.

On another occasion I overheard Evans helping Moore down the long curling staircase. In conversation Moore always emphasised the definite and indefinite articles.

> Moore: 'Tell me about *The Good Companions*. It is not a very good book, people tell me.'
> Evans: 'Not a good book! We've already sold a hundred and fifty thousand copies.'

The firm's battery of living authors was impressive. *The Forsyte Saga* and *The Good Companions* were reprinted again and again, as was the volume of Masefield's *Collected Poems*, and Maurice Baring, Max

Beerbohm, Galsworthy, Edmund Gosse, Graham Greene, Margaret Kennedy, Masefield, Somerset Maugham, George Moore and Priestley composed a formidable front line.

[9]

1931 was a disastrous year for me, but it began agreeably enough. I had been to few concerts before, but now in January, encouraged by Peg, I attended ones given by Schnabel, Prokofiev, Kreisler, and Stravinsky, on which I commented 'Ansermet conducted with wicked ritual, like the Borgias' cook.'

I met T. E. Lawrence briefly in the Heinemann office, and was elected to the Garrick Club, proposed by Jamie Hamilton (now a publisher on his own) and seconded by Sir Johnston Forbes-Robertson.

Jamie Hamilton

I remained a happy member for forty years. Also I saw the Marx Brothers in the flesh at the Palace Theatre. Here are some extracts from my diary:

> *29 January.*   Read *Arms and the Man* again. I think it is piffle. Shaw is always so bloody pleased with himself, and thinks his own jokes so funny. I'm sure he is over-rated. Most of his plays are boring to see and to read. (Except for *St Joan* this is still my opinion.)
>
> *3 February.*   Enormously impressed by first night of Eugene O'Neill's *Strange Interlude.*
>
> *9 February.*   Columbus Party at Heinemann's to celebrate Priestley's first visit to America. It lasted from 9.30 p.m. to 2 a.m. Hardly sat down – played butler in the hall, circulated drinks and was photographed talking to various authors. The waiters got quite blotto and refused to leave. Priestley in wonderful form.
>
> *10 February.*   No word of praise or thanks from Evans. Only a lecture about being 'on the job'.
>
> *14 February.*   Last night of *The Breadwinner.*

[10]

From February 17 to 21 Peg played the part of Pervaneh in Flecker's *Hassan* in an unsatisfactory performance by the O.U.D.S. Peg's performance was beautiful, but most of the undergraduates, especially the one who played her lover, were incapable of reproducing the richness of Flecker's prose and verse.

There then followed three West End failures, the first of which introduced us to a most remarkable man. It was called *Charles the Third*, adapted by Edgar Wallace from a literal translation of the German. The whole play was set in a convent, with many walking-on nuns, Peg as a novice wrongly believed pregnant, and Ronald Squire, who doubled the parts of an aged Cardinal and his illegitimate grandson.

After the dress rehearsal, which hadn't gone too well, I was sitting in Peg's dressing-room with her friend Diana Wynyard. Suddenly the door burst open and in strode Wallace, wearing his hat, smoking a cigarette in a long holder, and with a face of thunder. 'Those bloody nuns are no good; they'll have to go,' he said fiercely. Somewhat haltingly I introduced him to Diana, who didn't catch his name, and astonishingly, since his appearance was as well known as the King's, failed to recognise him. 'How did you like the show, Miss Wynyard?'

he asked aggressively. 'Very much,' she said, 'but I think it's an insult to be asked to stand to attention when the National Anthem is played by a machine.' Wallace had just installed in the theatre a panatrope, the most up-to-date and expensive kind of gramophone. 'Good evening, Miss Wynyard,' he growled, and left the room.

We spent the next week-end at his house overlooking the Thames near Bourne End. In the middle of Sunday morning, when he was sitting in the drawing-room, gloomily playing Corinthian Bagatelle, with hat and cigarette-holder in position, he suddenly said: 'By God that girl's right.' A footman was sent to fetch Wallace's manager Bill Linnit, and when he arrived panting, Wallace said: 'Which is the biggest bloody theatre orchestra in London?' 'Perhaps the Lyceum,' said Linnit. 'Right,' said Wallace: 'hire it to start tomorrow night,' and went on with his game. Somehow the wretched Linnit scrambled together a number of orchestral players, and they duly started work next evening, but their employment was brief, as the play closed on Saturday.

At this time Wallace's income was enormous (he had published some sixty books and written sixteen plays in the previous five years), but he squandered his fortune in the theatre, on the racecourse, and by his immense generosity to the needy. The household in the country consisted of his second wife Jim and his three younger children, who treated him with a mixture of awe and tolerant affection. They called him Krazy, after a cartoon cat. There were numerous servants, including relays of footmen, ready to bring him a cup of tea at any moment of the day or night. He looked unhealthily flabby, with a grey face. At meals he drank only orange squash, smoked most of the time, and delighted us with splendid stories. I have listened to many *raconteurs*, and he was the best of all – a natural storyteller of genius.

We asked if we could see him at work, and he readily agreed. His novel *The Man at the Carlton* was being serialised in the *Daily Express*, and owing to his other commitments – racing, theatrical and journalistic – he was only twenty-four hours ahead of the serialisation. Wearing his famous dressing-gown he switched on the dictaphone, into which he spoke all his books (except for plays, which he wrote with a pen), and started hesitantly, having forgotten the characters' names. After a few minutes of rambling narrative, he said into the machine: 'Cut out all that and start again'. By then he was back in the groove, and the complicated story flowed from him without pause or hesitation. When he switched off at the end of the chapter I asked him whether it was true that, as a boy selling newspapers in the street, he had kept himself warm by reciting Shakespeare. 'Perfectly true,' he said, switched on the machine, and began my old favourite, 'Oh pardon me, thou bleeding piece of earth, That I am meek and gentle with these butchers' – and on, word-perfect, to the end of Antony's speech. Very confusing, no doubt, for his ace-typist Bob Curtis, but I daresay he was used to such interpolations. Determined to get ahead of the serial, Wallace worked through Sunday night, and when we left after breakfast on Monday we took with us cylinders containing seven thousand words, which we delivered to Curtis in London.

At this time Wallace edited, and largely wrote, a tabloid weekly newspaper called the *Sunday News*. Certainly the racing, theatrical, gossip and leader pages were entirely his, and he sometimes used them to pay off old scores. Of the critic Hannen Swaffer, who he considered had let him down, he wrote, roughly in these words: 'Good old Swaff. I rejoice in his success. When I first knew him he hadn't a penny, and now he must be earning every bit of ten thousand a year.' Knowing the victim, I said to Wallace: 'Surely he can't be earning anything like that.' 'Of course not,' he answered, 'but it may provoke some awkward questions from the Inland Revenue.' When he discovered that Maurice Browne had given Peg an iniquitous contract by which she received sixteen pounds a week for Desdemona, and for the next two years half of anything she earned over sixteen pounds was to go to Browne, he wrote to Browne saying that unless he cancelled the contract immediately the whole of it would be printed in the *Sunday News*. Browne capitulated by return of post.

Later Wallace took us in his yellow Rolls Royce to a race-meeting at Hurst Park. When we arrived all the paper-boys surrounded the car crying 'God bless you, Mr Wallace,' and he threw them half-crowns as largesse. He insisted on backing a horse for us in every race, but none of them was even placed. A few months later he died in Hollywood, a burnt-out meteor of incredible brilliance.

[11]

I had by now realised that, despite Evans's vague protestations, there was no future for me at Heinemann's, so I once more called on Jamie Hamilton to find me a job elsewhere. He tackled his old boss Jonathan Cape, who seemed interested. I was introduced to his partner G. Wren

(Bob) Howard and the junior director Piers Gilchrist Thompson, who showed me over Cape's imposing offices at 30 Bedford Square.

One day I was rung up at Heinemann's by Barbara Back, whom I had met with Somerset Maugham. She asked me if I would like a job as assistant literary editor of the *Spectator*. I said no, but I had a friend Peter Fleming who would be just the man for the job. So began Peter's association with the paper, which lasted, on and off, for the rest of his life.

My diary continues:

29 February. Taken by a friend to William Michael Rossetti's old house in St Edmund's Terrace, where his crippled daughter proudly showed us her collection of Pre-Raphaelite pictures. Thrilled to hear her referring to 'my Aunt Christina' and 'my Uncle Dante Gabriel.' Then sat on Shelley's sofa, on which he is supposed to have spent his last night on earth. All rather claustrophobic but very touching.

3 March. Gave Charlie Marford dinner at the Café Royal, then back to the flat. He without job or money but cheerful as ever.

7 March. Talked to Max Beerbohm at Heinemann's.

8 March. Lunched with William Nicholson and his wife Edie, who invited me to visit them at Sutton Veny.

13 May. Lunched with Walter de la Mare and family. He talked of English words and their suitability to describe the things they stood for. 'Gas a bad word, Ether a good one.'

19 May. Talked to Evans about leaving. He asked me to stay ten days.

20 May. Charlie and Molly to supper, after which he did brilliant imitations of all the leading actors he had played with, ending with his exit-line in a preposterous play set in the eighteenth century:

'Don't be a fool, Gideon Bloodgood. 'Twas not I who put the infernal machine into the ship's hold.'

6 June. First night of Peg's second failure – a play translated from the Dutch of a delightful old playwright called Jan Fabricius.

8 June. Final interview with Evans, who turned on the charm.

11 June. Left Heinemann's for good.

12 June. Visited Priestley in his Hampstead home and talked for an hour and a half. He promised to look out for a job for me.

13 June.   Last night of Peg's play.

16 June.   With Peg to see the Compagnie des Quinze in André Obey's *Noé*, directed by Michel Saint-Denis. All through the play Noah talked to God, and when the Ark had landed safely he looked up and cried out '*Seigneur, es tu content?*', and as the curtain slowly fell a rainbow appeared in the sky.

17 June.   Paul came round and sang Mozart, Schubert, Quilter, and Russian songs. Lovely.

18 June.   With Peg to Obey's *Viol de Lucrèce*, which is the best thing I have seen in any theatre for years. The play is a fine one, the individual performances excellent, the production and *ensemble* beyond all praise. Everything they do is to a pattern, all orchestrated and timed to perfection. One mood holds them all. They seem unable to make a mistake. The effect is of a symphony. In the interval visited the Priestleys in their box and was introduced to Hugh Walpole.

30 June.   First night of Peg's third failure, *Sea Fever*, translated from the French of Marcel Pagnol. It closed on 4 July.

[12]

And then, alas, our happy and short-lived marriage gradually began to fall apart. As I wrote to George Lyttelton almost thirty years later, 'My love for Peggy, which will be with me always, was (I now see) chiefly an intellectual and spiritual passion, tied up with poetry and music, drama, youth and spring. Basically it wasn't a physical passion at all, which is why the marriage foundered.' As Iris Origo wrote in her *Images and Shadows*, concerning the early courtship of her parents: 'It was, at this stage, almost entirely an attraction of the mind, as sexless and yet intense as only the ardour of the very young and very intelligent can sometimes be.' But there were other minor troubles. Husband working all day and wife all evening produce what are now called 'unsocial hours'. Also simulated love-making on the stage often turns to the real thing off-stage, and, except for Sybil Thorndike, the private lives of the great actresses have seldom run smoothly, since they are in fact forever wedded to the theatre.

Be all that as it may, our separation was agonising, with many tears on both sides. Peg left the flat and I was alone, filled with sorrow and shame at being such a failure as a husband, and with no job to occupy my time. I hadn't even the heart to continue writing my diary, an omission which I now greatly regret.

I accepted the Nicholsons' invitation and spent some time at Sutton Veny, where they lent me a snug little cottage. Across the fields in a farm-house oddly named The Poulk lived Nicholson's daughter Nancy with her four children and her lover Geoffrey Taylor (né Phibbs), a wild, intelligent, witty and generous Irish poet. Nancy was married to Robert Graves, but as an extreme feminist she refused to be called Mrs Graves and remained Nancy Nicholson always. Her two sons were called Graves, her two daughters Nicholson. I loved all of them and visited them often. Despite my protestations Geoffrey gave me several valuable books. One day a dead rat was found in their water-supply. 'Oh well,' said Nancy, 'it's all nourishment.'

Later in the summer I spent a happy holiday with the Nicholsons near Letterfrack on the coast of Connemara. Edie and her three children, John and Anne Stuart-Wortley, whose father had been killed in the war, and Nicholson's daughter Liza, then always called Penny, went ahead, while William and I followed, sharing a cabin on the boat. At Dublin we found a telegram from Edie saying HOUSE GAUNT BUT CLEAN. 'Do you think the same could be said of us?' asked William. I had persuaded him to spend a night in Dublin because Charlie and Molly were working there in the Gate Theatre. We were introduced to Micheál MacLiammóir and Hilton Edwards who were joint actor-managers. Micheál, one of the most remarkable and gifted men I have ever known, later became a great friend. I couldn't help noticing a beautiful little Irish colleen with black hair and blue eyes. Her name was Betty Chancellor.

In Connemara William painted a portrait of me in a blue-and-white-striped jersey, sitting on a rocking-chair. The picture disappeared, believed to have been stolen from William's London studio. John rocked a great deal on the chair, and William said: 'Thank God it isn't a rocking sofa'. I loved to watch William painting this picture and others. Edie, who was serious-minded, eagerly searched for different kinds of moss along the shore. On one such walk William suddenly stooped and picked up a fragment, calling out 'This is the kind of moss that grows on Grandfather'. Edie was not amused.

One day we were told that Augustus John was staying in a grand hotel along the shore, and we set out in a vain attempt to find him. When we got stuck in a thicket behind the hotel, William said: 'The

William Nicholson

great thing is to remember the old adage "Follow the drains and you come to the bathing-place." ' He made everything fun.

Back in London I found life very dull, although negotiations with Cape were nearing completion, so I went back to Dublin to see more of Charlie and Molly. They had been living in an unconverted signal-box with no domestic conveniences. The strain of this, coupled with a lot of rehearsing and acting, culminated in Čapek's *R.U.R.*, the first play in which most of the characters are robots. This was too much for Molly, who suffered a nervous breakdown, haunted and terrified by phantasmal robots. She was recovering in hospital when I arrived and I visited her every day.

I spent much time in the theatre, where one day a grandiloquent American teenager turned up and asked for an audition. They were looking for an actor to play the important part of the Duke in *Jew Süss* and asked him to declaim it from the script. They were so impressed with his potential power that they let him play the part, in which he gave an outstanding performance. His name was Orson Welles.

Charlie was still living in the signal-box and doing a lot of scene-painting, mostly from designs of Micheál's. He was constantly pursued by a horrible young woman who was said to have nits in her hair. At a party on the stage she had too much to drink, collapsed on the stage and was violently sick. Charlie said: 'There's not much left of the mystery of womanhood when that one's puking all over you.' Orson Welles said: 'Don't step on it. It may be Lon Chaney.'

I lived in digs, two large and gloomy rooms in Herbert Street, where I saw a lot of Betty Chancellor, with whom I fell deeply in love. She, bless her, returned my affection, but I told her there was no future in it, since I was married and had no job. We parted tearfully, and some time later she married the Irish playwright Denis Johnston, by whom she had two sons.

When Molly had completely recovered I accompanied her and Charlie to Llandudno on the North Wales coast and spent a week with them there in cosy theatrical digs. In those days a double room in such digs was called a 'combined chat', a phrase which not even Charlie could explain. We spent hours in gramophone shops, playing records which we seldom if ever bought, going to one of the cinemas, for which Charlie got us free seats by showing his theatrical card, and walking on the wintry sea-front. Those were very happy days.

Arrangements with Cape were almost completed when I was suddenly offered a job in the Book Society, probably at Priestley's suggestion. I went to see Cape and suggested that I should accept the job for a year, after which I should know a great deal more about books, authors and publishers, and therefore be of greater value to him. He agreed, so I faced 1932, if not with a song in my heart, at least with two jobs under my belt.

[13]

The Book Society, which opened its doors in 1929, employed a Selection Committee of five literary people who each month chose a book (The Book Society Choice) which they thought outstanding, and

With Charlie and Molly at Llandudno

recommended a further half-dozen books. Reviews of all these by the Selection Committee were sent to members each month in a paper called the *Book Society News*. The founder and manager of the whole concern was Alan Bott, an accomplished journalist and author. He was a dour man but could be reduced to helpless giggles by his enchanting and very amusing wife Jo. (He later started Pan Books.) He was so concerned that the management might be accused of influencing the choice of books on monetary grounds that he had no contact with the Selection Committee, and I was the only person from the office who attended their monthly meetings.

Before I started work there Priestley took me out to tea and described the Committee to me thus: 'Hugh wants to choose every book. I want to choose no book. Sylvia Lynd wants to choose books by people with whom she has dinner. George Gordon (President of Magdalen College, Oxford) is too busy to read the books, but his wife reads them for him. And as for Clemence Dane, she takes a pre-Caxton view of books, and the sight of print on the page excites her to madness.' I found there was a considerable amount of truth in what he said, but by the time I started work Priestley had retired from the Committee and been replaced by Edmund Blunden.

After spending a night in Oxford to see Peg's first Juliet, with Christopher Hassall as Romeo, Edith Evans as the Nurse and John Gielgud as director, I took over my job from Arthur Barker, who was leaving to start his own publishing business, and for a week or two he sat with me to put me in the picture. The first thing Alan told me to do was to visit every leading publisher in London and make myself known to them. They were all very nice to me, except for Douglas Jerrold, the head of Eyre & Spottiswoode, who sneeringly said that he couldn't imagine why I should want to work for such a dishonest firm. The 'dishonesty', I discovered, was the fact that no book of his firm's had so far been chosen. Nor was his treatment of me likely to favour his cause.

The Selection Committee met in Hugh Walpole's flat at 90 Piccadilly, in which the sitting-room had a fine view across the Green Park to Buckingham Palace. Arthur Barker came with me and showed me exactly what to do. This momentous meeting introduced me to Edmund, who became one of my dearest friends, and re-introduced me to Hugh, who was to be the greatest benefactor of my life.

The book chosen that day was a novel called *The Soldier and the Gentlewoman* by Hilda Vaughan, the wife of Charles Morgan, and published by Victor Gollancz. When we came out from the meeting Arthur said, 'We might as well ring up Victor and tell him the good news,' which he did from a call-box. 'Victor says we're to go round to his office.' It was after office-hours, and Victor was in an awful windowless loose-box at the back of the ground floor in Henrietta Street, Covent Garden. In the front office a lady of uncertain age was hovering to let us in.

Victor burst out of his room. 'Is the book definitely chosen?'

'Yes.'

'Very well. Miss Something, *Release Those Bands*' (in a voice of thunder).

The poor woman opened a huge drawer, in which were millions of bands saying CHOSEN BY THE BOOK SOCIETY, which Victor had clearly had printed in large quantity, since they would do for any book. It was so patently obvious that the wretched woman couldn't possibly do anything with the bands that evening that we simply gasped with admiration at this splendid piece of gamesmanship (though that word hadn't yet been coined). Victor then took us across to the Savoy and ordered a magnum of champagne, which the three of us drank to the book's success. The whole thing was done to impress me, and impress me it did. Accustomed to the aridities of Heinemann, I thought, 'This is publishing. This is life!'

Some years later Guy Chapman used exactly the same words describing how his early boss, the somewhat unconventional Scottish publisher T. Werner Laurie, took him to lunch at the Royal Automobile Club. When they collected their hats and coats afterwards Laurie asked the hat-check girl: 'Are you going to sleep with me tonight, darling?' 'Indeed I am *not*, Mr Laurie. You almost tore me in half last time.' Guy's thoughts and words were exactly mine.

My job consisted of getting all likely books from the more-than-willing publishers and distributing them to the Selection Committee. If one of them let me know of a book he or she thought a possible choice I made sure the others read it. I also edited the *Book Society News*, whose size and format I improved, and solicited advertisements from publishers.

The next Choice but one was Graham Greene's fourth novel *Stamboul Train*. His first three had received good reviews but sold only a thousand or two. This Choice sent his sales rocketing to 20,000, and he never looked back. For a long time Graham believed that I had been responsible for the Choice, although I told him I had only made sure they all read it. Anyhow he generously gave me the corrected typescript of the book, which, years later when I was very hard up, I sold with his permission.

Hugh Walpole was fond of Clemence Dane, but he was irritated by her because, after almost every meeting, she left her umbrella or some other object in his flat. Her real name was Winifred Ashton, and we all knew and loved her as Winifred. Hugh spent a week-end in her house at Hunthay, near Axminster in Devon. He told me that she took him for a walk through some water-meadows, where the water flooded his shoes and socks. There came a point when, he said, he suddenly felt that nothing would ever make him stay there again.

A few weeks later I spent a week-end at Hunthay, and on Sunday morning Winifred came crashing down the stairs, carrying six books submitted to the Book Society, which she had taken up the night before and, in a manner, read. After breakfast she took me for that same walk, and at a certain point she said: 'I took Hugh for this walk, and just here I saw a look on his face as much as to say: "Whatever happens I can never come here again".' I longed to congratulate her on the exactitude of her extra-sensory perception, but forbore.

Hugh had a stalwart man to look after him, a Cornishman called Harold Cheevers, who had served in the Navy and after the war became a London policeman. He was once revolver champion of the British Isles and was a fine swimmer. He was married with two sons. Hugh bought them a house in Hampstead, in which Hugh often took refuge during the beginning of the Blitz. Harold was a large man – not tall or fat but sturdy and massive – with fair hair and blue eyes. The outstanding traits of his character were shrewd common sense, unswerving integrity, and an imperturbability which was only increased by the excitable enthusiasms of Hugh and others. He drove and maintained Hugh's car, kept his cheque-book and was always with him, even in Hollywood.

At Brackenburn when they were alone they ate together in the dining-room, but if there were visitors Harold ate with the servants, Jack and Edith. Hugh used to tease him by asking his opinion of visitors after they had left, and when Harold had reluctantly said: 'He seemed a good fellow' or something of the sort, the next time Hugh saw the person he would say 'Do you know what Harold said about you?' and then tell him.

But once Harold outwitted him, after the visit of Clemence Dane. She was a large woman, overflowing with talent as writer, painter and sculptor, good and generous to all. In appearance a long dress always masked her large bosom and descended to hidden immensities below. When asked what he had thought of her Harold refused to answer, until Hugh, by repeating the question again and again, got Harold to say 'She'd strip awkward'. Every time I saw the dear lady afterwards the terrible truth of Harold's words was borne in on me.

Harold always carried a little revolver in his jacket-pocket. One blackout night in the Blitz he was walking down Piccadilly to Hugh's flat, when a tipsy American G.I. tripped over the kerb and fell flat on his face. As Harold stepped forward to help him, the G.I. leapt up, faced Harold and said: 'I've got a gun. Gimme your wallet.' This was the moment for which Harold had been waiting. He took out his revolver and with his left hand flashed his torch on to it, saying: 'You aren't the only so-and-so who carries a gun'. The G.I., who was unarmed, said 'Okay, buddy, you win' and held out his wallet to Harold, who refused to take it.

One Sunday at Brackenburn I asked Harold to show me what he could do with a revolver. The only tiny target I could find on Hugh's desk was a visiting-card of Miss G.B. Stern, a successful novelist, friend of Hugh's and mine. I stuck it on a tall bush across the lawn, and with one shot Harold put a bullet exactly through the middle of it. I pocketed the card and told Harold that when my body was dragged out of the crash of the night-express this relic would need some explaining.

[14]

One day in early summer Alan Bott sent for me and told me that next day Heinemann's were giving a big garden-party at Kingswood. He was too busy to go, but if I would take his wife Jo there and back I could have the day off. Nothing could have been more agreeable. Jo was always an enchanting companion, full of jokes and unexpectedness.

The first thing I saw when we got there was a trio of the firm's leading authors standing arm-in-arm to be photographed, and they might have been an illustration of the British class-system – Priestley a no-nonsense North Country plebeian; Galsworthy a member of the *haute bourgeoisie*, every inch a Forsyte; and Cunninghame Graham, pride of the Scottish aristocracy.

Then, having lost sight of Jo, I struggled through the crowd until I saw a fair-haired girl sitting alone under a tree. Thinking she was Daphne du Maurier, I approached her and introduced myself. She told me her name was Comfort Borden-Turner, that her mother was the novelist Mary Borden, and that she was working in Heinemann's London office as a typist. We talked happily for some time and she agreed to have lunch with me in the near future. The power of chance had struck again.

[15]

Our friendship blossomed quickly. The Piccadilly flat was a handy place for meeting, and before long we became joyful lovers. She told me that if we married I should have two lots of in-laws. Her mother, the novelist, came from a rich American family, their wealth obtained

Comfort

from Borden's Milk of Chicago. When she was in her late teens her grandmother took her round the world. In India they met a gentle Scottish lay-missionary called George Douglas Turner. He fell deeply in love with the beautiful young heiress, proposed to her and was accepted. They were married and their first two daughters were born in India – Joyce in 1909, Comfort in 1910. Then they descended upon England, where they soon acquired a large London house and a larger one in the country. This did not suit Douglas, and he escaped to the Balkan Wars, where he served for several years. Their third daughter Emmy was born before the opening of the Great War.

In 1914 Douglas joined the regular army, in which he had several jobs in army intelligence. The one he was proudest of was when he was sent to calm down a New Zealand contingent who showed signs of mutiny. He ended his short speech of exhortation by saying 'Lord Macaulay imagined in the far future a visitor from New Zealand, standing on a broken arch of London Bridge and viewing the ruins of St Paul's. *You* are going to do a much more wonderful thing. You are going to stand on a broken arch of the Hohenzollern Bridge across the Rhine and view the ruins of Cologne'. They cheered him for minutes and went off happy.

Meanwhile Mary Borden (or May, as she was called by family and friends) was financing and running her own field-hospital with the French Army. One day a handsome young wounded British officer was carried into her hospital, and nursing him turned to love on both sides. As soon as he was convalescent she temporarily handed over the hospital to her second-in-command and eloped with her patient. His name was Louis Spears. His origins were obscure, his parents never mentioned. He spoke French like a Frenchman, and English with a slight French accent.

In 1918 Douglas divorced her and she married Spears. There was a prolonged legal wrangle about the custody of the three children, but Douglas finally agreed that they should live with their mother, with regular visits to him. After the war he was secretary to Lord Robert Cecil at the Peace Conference, then an Oxford don, a prison governor, and finally an Inspector of Prisons appointed by the Home Office. Once, when he visited Dartmoor there was a riot in progress and he was hustled away by prison officers. For years afterwards he was approached in various streets by loiterers and malcontents who always said: 'Remember me, sir? I was the man who saved your life at Dartmoor.' When an Inspector called, any prisoner could be granted an interview with him. One man complained about the prison library.

'Are you fond of reading?'

'Yes, sir, very fond.'

'Who is your favourite author?'

'William Shakespeare, sir.'

'Oh, what did he write?'

Long pause.

'*The Coachman's Waistcoat*, sir.'

'Anything else?'

'No, sir. Just *The Coachman's Waistcoat*.'

Pop and Margaret

When I first met Douglas, whom his children called Pop, he was happily married to an American novelist called Margaret Wilson who had met him in India, loved him then and forever after. They had a flat in Woburn Square, Bloomsbury and a delightful little house called Church Gates at Blockley in Gloucestershire.

Meanwhile the Spears family had a grand house in Lord North Street, Westminster, a large house in Kent and a yacht. Spears retired from the Army as a Brigadier with a Military Cross and a host of foreign decorations. He was National Liberal Member of Parliament for Loughborough 1922–24, and Conservative Member for Carlisle 1931–45. They had a son, who was a happy little schoolboy when I first saw him, but he fell victim to osteomyelitis, and for the rest of his short life was ill and unhappy.

In 1929–30 the Borden family (with one exception) lost all their money in the Wall Street crash. The yacht was sold. Lord North Street gave way to a rather poky little house on the edge of Mayfair, the Kentish mansion to a modest little house near Bracknell in Berkshire. So strong was May's character that nobody meeting her for the first time after the disaster could guess that she had once been very rich and was now rather poor.

While I was courting Comfort I disingenuously asked my Uncle Duff if he knew a man called Spears in the House of Commons. Duff answered, 'If he had the word SHIT written on his forehead in letters

Comfort at Cancale

of fire it wouldn't be more apparent than it is now. He's the most unpopular man in the House. Don't trust him: he'll let you down in the end.' This prophecy was fulfilled twenty years later.

On 16 June 1932 I saw Peter off at Tilbury on his crackpot journey to South America.[1] He and Celia had grown to love each other, and I promised to look after her as much as possible while he was away. Luckily she and Comfort had been together at St Paul's Girls School in London. Peter was away until October.

During my short summer holiday Comfort and I spent a happy week at Cancale, on the Brittany coast near St Malo. We were anxious not

[1] See his book *Brazilian Adventure* (1933) which made him famous as a writer.

to meet anyone we knew, so spent our time swimming, sun-bathing, making love and enjoying the oysters and fish for which the place was famous. Comfort spoke perfect French, having been to a *lycée* at an early age.

I told Peg I wanted a divorce, and, as was the custom in those days, offered to supply evidence of supposed adultery, so as to appear to be the guilty party. For the sake of Comfort and her family I wanted her to be left out of it, and luckily she produced a charming girl-friend who agreed to spend two nights with me in a bedroom in the Charing Cross Hotel for a fiver. This exercise was carried out successfully, with a good deal of laughter, but when we left on the second morning I had only three pounds left, which I shamefacedly gave my accomplice. I then lodged the hotel bill as evidence of adultery.

In the autumn Charlie came to stay in the flat, sleeping on the divan in the sitting-room, while Molly stayed with her family near Golders Green. Peg got him a walking-on part in Emil Ludwig's *Versailles*, which was all about the Peace Treaty of 1919. Charlie, who was a Bulgarian attaché or some such, was issued with a pair of knee-length Russian boots, which for the run of the play he wore everywhere. One day Eric Portman went to a matinée, and when the whole concourse of ministers and minions dried up, Eric heard Charlie's well-known voice saying: 'I'm sure somebody says something here'.

At the end of the year I sadly gave up the lease of the flat and moved to a seventeenth-century house, 11 Lawrence Street, Chelsea, where I occupied the first and second floors, while the ground-floor and basement housed a disagreeable couple who ran some sort of laundry.

[16]

1933 began with a crisis. In January Deirdre and Ronnie had taken the Villa Nueva, outside Palma in Majorca, and in February Comfort went out to stay with them. I was horrified to learn that her first love, a horrible young man, was on his way trying to snatch her from me. The only thing to do was to catch up with him. So, on 19 February I travelled to Marseilles by boat and train, then drove out to the airfield. The weather was atrocious, and they told me all flights had been cancelled, but a small two-seater mail-plane was going to attempt a flight to Barcelona. They agreed to put me in the back with the letters, gave me a paper bag to be sick into (which I didn't need), and we were off. We were buffeted about by gale-force winds, up, down, from side to side. Crossing the Pyrenees I was so certain I was going to be killed that I tore a blank page out of a book and wrote my will, though in fact I had nothing to leave except a few books. I have never been so frightened for so long at a stretch.

When we eventually came down at Barcelona, most of the runways were under water, and some of the staff were out shooting duck. I got a taxi to the port and caught a boat for Palma. On it I ran into the young man. He said: 'Now I see you here I've a good mind to go straight home.' I said: 'As far as I'm concerned you can go to hell.' I never saw him again.

After a couple of happy days with Comfort, I came home in a more leisurely fashion, but before I left I learned that the young man was staying in Palma, waiting for me to leave, so that he could have another go at Comfort. I was worried as to how I should handle the situation when she came home. On 2 March I lunched with the novelist Margaret Kennedy, one of the kindest and wisest people I knew, who had taken Clemence Dane's place on the Selection Committee. I told her the whole story and asked what she advised me to do. She said 'When she comes home meet her at the station, give her a kiss, put her in a taxi for her mother's house, and before it leaves tell her gently that if she doesn't promise never to see the young man again, she will never see *you* again. If she truly loves you she'll come back to you. If not, you'll be better off without her.' I followed this admirable advice exactly, and then endured days of agonising uncertainty. Finally after a week Comfort telephoned tearfully in the middle of the night to say she was coming back to me for good. On 23 March I wrote in my engagement-diary the words 'A Singing Bird', referring to Christina Rossetti's poem which begins 'My heart is like a singing bird' and ends 'Because my love is come to me'.

[17]

I left the Book Society at the end of March, and after some final bargaining with Jonathan Cape I joined him in April. He said I couldn't be a director of the firm until I had proved myself worthy. I told him that unless I joined as a director with his full confidence I wouldn't join at all. He capitulated unwillingly, and said: 'I can only offer you the salary of a Member of Parliament', which was then £600 a year. I tried to hide my delight, as this was much more than I had ever earned before. All along I had been buoyed up by an allowance of £300 a year from my father.

Jonathan Cape's family came from Cumberland, but he was born and spent all his life in London. Starting at sixteen as an errand-boy in Hatchard's Piccadilly bookshop, he worked his way up as traveller for Harper, then for Duckworth, of which he became Managing Director. He then held the same position in the Medici Society, where he made friends with a young Cambridge graduate called G. Wren (Bob) Howard, who showed signs of a gift for design and a good business sense. They realised there was no future for them where they were, so they decided to set up on their own, with £5000 borrowed from Howard's father and £7000 which Cape had made by publishing, as Page & Co, a shilling edition of novels by Elinor Glyn, which Duckworth had published originally. In future all profits, bonuses etc were divided five to Bob and seven to Jonathan.

Jonathan Cape

The firm of Jonathan Cape Ltd began on 1 January 1921 at 11 Gower Street, Bloomsbury, and their first publication was a nine-guinea reprint of C. M. Doughty's *Arabia Deserta*. This was a bold move, since the book had fallen flat when it was first published in 1888, but they knew how much T. E. Lawrence admired the book and they persuaded him to write a long introduction for nothing. As a result the book sold well, and they were off. In that same year Cape purchased the business of A. C. Fifield, which brought him the works of Samuel Butler and W. H. Davies.

Four years later they moved to an eighteenth-century mansion, 30 Bedford Square, where their rent was exactly balanced by what they charged a firm of surveyors for the two top floors. I had a nice little room on the first floor, looking over the square, and a secretary of my own.

Jonathan was fifty-four when I joined him, and he taught me almost everything I ever knew about publishing. After his death Eric Linklater described him accurately as 'a publisher of outstanding genius with the heart of a horse-coper'. When Eric's third novel *Juan in America* was a Book Society Choice Jonathan immediately travelled to Edinburgh, where Eric was living, bearing a contract that would bind Eric to him for another three years, and assuring him that a ten per cent royalty was as much as anyone could expect. As insurance against a bad year, all salaries were kept as low as possible, and a profitable year produced bonuses for directors and staff. Jonathan was much easier to work for than Charley Evans, willing to delegate without bothering about his thunder being stolen. Even before I joined him I persuaded him to give Peter Fleming a contract with a £300 advance for his book on Brazil before the expedition had started. He knew nothing of Peter but trusted my opinion.

Bob Howard was, if possible, a meaner man than Jonathan. His designing of all the firm's books gave them a reputation for good production, but Bob had a few quirks in his character. He paid little attention to other people, disliked almost all authors, considering them an unnecessary nuisance, and, even as some deeply religious people dislike discussing their beliefs, Bob's deep love of money prevented his ever mentioning it in any personal connection. The three of us met at 9 o'clock every morning in the boardroom and spent an hour opening the post and discussing everything. Authors' royalties and other financial matters came under review, but on the rare occasions when I was due for a rise in salary or a bonus, Bob was incapable of telling me so

Daniel George

by word of mouth, but sent his secretary right across the building with the good news in a hand-written note.

The dust-jackets, advertising and publicity were most effectively managed by a charming girl called Ruth Atkinson. One of the authors with whom I made great friends was Daniel George. His surname was Bunting, but he used his two Christian names for his verse, anthologies and multifarious reviewing. Cape published nine of his books in the 1930s. Born in 1890, he was a versatile man, having, before he turned to writing and editing, worked in a library, served as a rifleman in the war, invented disc-wheels for motor-cars, sold gas appliances and managed an engineering firm. He had always read prodigiously, and now he devoted himself to literature, and we often went book-hunting together. Then, as death and war-service claimed the editorial staff one by one, Daniel did an immense amount of reading and editing for the firm, in conjunction with Veronica Wedgwood, whose early books Cape had published.

But the person to whom I took an immediate and lasting liking was the firm's reader Edward Garnett. He was sixty-five when I met him, and he had been a publisher's reader for most of his life, having discovered Joseph Conrad, John Galsworthy, D. H. Lawrence and many other successful writers. William Plomer wrote of him: 'It does seem to me that Garnett's activities as a publisher's reader and as the friend and adviser of writers made him creative in a special sense – far more creative, I consider, than most writers.'

He was a shaggy-looking man, with grey hair coming forward in a fringe above his spectacles, jowly cheeks and untidy clothes. He had an impish sense of humour and a delightful way with words. When he praised some book and I gently said that it was unsaleable, he said, looking sternly at me over his spectacles: 'Always remember, my young friend, that there is still in this country a residuum of educated folk.'

Edward Garnett

All the manuscripts submitted to the firm were piled up for him to examine every Wednesday, after he had attended the directors' weekly lunch at the Etoile restaurant in Charlotte Street. He picked out half-a-dozen or more possibles, which the firm delivered to his flat in Pond Place off the Fulham Road. E. G. read them all, and then, in an astonishing feat of memory, wrote detailed reports on them all at the end of the week in the Underground on his way to Bedford Square. He and Jonathan always disliked each other, but each had a deep respect, Jonathan for E. G.'s literary flair, E. G. for Jonathan's publishing ability. E. G. couched all his reports in the royal or editorial 'we', and often introduced such a dig as: 'We cannot understand why Cape persists with this third-rate writer' (one of Jonathan's favourites). At the weekly lunch E. G. and I were often rebuked by Jonathan for talking about Edward Thomas or some other writer E. G. had known, instead of taking part in the firm's conversation. After lunch E. G. and I always walked back to the office, stopping on the way at Frank Norman's secondhand bookshop. He did most of his business with scientific and technical books for foreign universities, bought many big lots at auctions, and anything in them that wasn't scientific or technical was in the shop at a very low price. E. G. knew every book of the last fifty years: he bought a few books, I a great many.

Soon I discovered many more treasures when Edmund Blunden introduced me to the book-barrows on the Farringdon Road. There were eight of them, two of which were devoted to sixpenny and shilling books. We took brief-cases, even small suitcases, to carry home our finds, which we then discussed in a pub on the corner of Caledonian Road. Edmund's knowledge of books, authors and their handwriting was far wider and more encyclopaedic than E. G.'s, covering all the nineteenth and part of the eighteenth century, and he had a dowser's instinct for digging out treasures. He was then working on the *Nation*, had divorced his first wife and was being strenuously courted by a small Armenian girl with a grating voice, called Sylva Norman (originally Nahabedian), whom he later married.

My other favourite in the office was Hamish Miles, a short, slim, elegant man, full of intelligence and wit. He was an accomplished journalist, and when Cape acquired Desmond MacCarthy's monthly paper *Life and Letters* he engaged Hamish to edit it, to help E. G. with the manuscripts, and do other editorial work. But he was mainly known as one of the best translators of French books, particularly those of André Maurois. He found that Maurois spoke and wrote faultless

Hamish Miles

English, and only once did Hamish catch him out. When he was translating Maurois's life of Byron he spent some time at Newstead, checking the place-names, which had sometimes been Frenchified. He traced them all except a road called *la voie nuptiale*, and it wasn't until the very end of his stay that he realised it stood for bridle-path.

Hamish subscribed to the French right-wing-royalist paper, *Action Française*, because he so much enjoyed the wit and savagery of its two proprietors, Charles Maurras and Léon Daudet. He used to pass the paper on to me, and our favourite issue was the one in which they referred to the left-wing French Prime Minister Léon Bloy as '*cette girafe bissexuelle*'.

One of our most difficult jobs, which we often did together, was writing 'blurbs' for dust-jackets and the firm's list. General books were comparatively easy to summarise, but novels were tricky. One couldn't give away too much of the plot, or use superlatives which reviewers could slam without reading the book. All this was difficult enough if one had read manuscript or proof, but our real test came when Jonathan insisted on a blurb for the new novel which Miss E. H. Young was just about to write, so that booksellers could order copies well in advance. Not a word of the book was written and it had no title. All we knew was that the story was set in the same place as some of the author's earlier novels. After a great deal of discussion and several failures we succeeded in concocting a blurb which could have described any of the author's works. My favourite phrase in it was 'the criss-cross of affections in Upper Radstowe', which we thought would cover anything. To our delight our work was accepted by Miss Young and Jonathan, and finally appeared unaltered on the dust-jacket of the published book. That year I sent Hamish a Christmas card of two beautiful girls in a garden, on which I wrote 'With love from the Misses Mallett' (the heroines and title of one of Miss Young's earlier novels); others were called *William, The Curate's Wife, The Vicar's Daughter* and *Jenny Wren*. In return Hamish sent me this letter, deliberately mis-spelling my name:

Christmas Day   *Heyshott*

Dear Mr Hart-Davies, I have no doubt your intentions were excellent in sending me the so-called 'Christmas' card which reached here this morning. But I am *surprised* that a man-of-the-world like yourself should have chosen such a time to remind me of an episode in my life which I, for one, have long regarded as closed. Upper Radstowe knows me no more; and I sincerely hope that the curate's wife, the vicar's daughter, the Misses Mallett, Miss Wren, and William (whom I treated very badly in these quiet streets) have one and all forgiven and forgotten these extravagances of my romantic and buried youth. I must say that this portrait of the younger Miss Mallett (reclining) is particularly good. But I should really prefer that you do not again disturb my emotional tranquillity in this poignant way. Believe me,
                        Yours truly, H. MILES
                                    Pres. of Royal Blurbological Society
                                                                    etc.

Hamish always supplied a much needed *leit-motif* in the office, and I became very fond of him, but at the end of 1937, just when he had secured a post on *The Times*, he died suddenly of a brain-tumour, aged forty-three. I missed him sorely.

[18]

In June I spent my first week-end with Hugh Walpole in his house Brackenburn, which looked over Lake Derwentwater and was stuffed with books, new and old.

Despite the law's delays my divorce was slowly proceeding on its way when Peg telephoned in some distress to say that she was living with the Russian director Theodore Komisarjevsky, and couldn't possibly appear as the innocent party, so I took steps to reverse the action, asking for the Court's discretion for my two nights in the Charing Cross Hotel, and the dreary process continued until I was eventually called to give evidence in the Law Courts. In those days Divorce was lumped together in one division with Admiralty and Probate, and before my case we had to sit through an Admiralty one. It concerned a collision on the Thames, and the Judge was Mr Justice Langton. He spoke his summing-up in clear and beautiful English, without apparently looking at his notes. An old sea-dog had obviously been bribed to say that a moored barge had drifted two hundred yards against the tide, and when the Judge came to him he said: 'We now come to the evidence of Captain X. This I find probable neither as fact nor as fiction, and since moreover it is in direct contradiction to the laws of nature I propose to discountenance it' – a sentence of which Doctor Johnson would surely have approved. The Decree Nisi was granted, but we had to wait another six months for the Decree Absolute.

In August Ronnie telephoned to say that Deirdre was dangerously ill, so I once again set out on the long journey to Majorca, on a calmer route than my first one. By the time I arrived she was better, but I decided to stay till she was out of danger. I spent a lot of time swimming in the sea. One day the orange-boats came in from Spain, and when they had sold all they could they tipped the rest of their cargoes into the water. The wind changed and the whole sea in front of the Villa Nueva was thickly covered with bobbing oranges. It was fun swimming through them, for they weren't rotten and smelt delicious.

On 20 November the Decree was made Absolute, and five days later Comfort and I were married in the Chelsea Register Office, with Deirdre (well again) and Peter (back from Brazil) as our witnesses. That evening we had a happy party in Lawrence Street.

[19]

1934 began with an enjoyable week's honeymoon in Paris. Duff and Diana took us out to lunch and gave us snails to eat, which we did our best to enjoy. Between theatres, picture-galleries and bookshops we visited two author-friends of Comfort's mother. One was André Maurois, who received us warmly and inscribed for us copies of his Proustian pastiche *Le Côté de Chelsea* and his life of Edward VII. The other friend was the enchanting Princesse Marie Murat, who gave us

Honeymoon in Paris

several of her books and told us how, on her way to Proust's funeral, she met at the bus-stop her old aunt from the country.

'*Ou vas-tu, Marie?*'

'*Je vais à l'enterrement de Marcel Proust.*'

'*Qui était ce Marcel Proust?*'

Et puis je me sentais une immense fatigue, car je savais
que je ne pouvais jamais expliquer à ma tante ce que
c'était Marcel Proust, et alors je lui ai dit:

'*C'était un jardinier qui faisait très bien son métier.*'

[20]

In the spring Comfort delightedly found that she was pregnant. We quickly realised that Lawrence Street would not do for a baby, and once again the power of chance was manifested. Even as Peg's and my dinner with the Lavers had resulted in the discovery of 213 Piccadilly, so did a lunch with the writer Richard Hughes and his wife produce our next home, since they were leaving and we took over their lease. 21 Lloyd Square was and is a Georgian terrace house on the south-west boundary of Islington, above Mount Pleasant post-office. The house contained three floors and a basement, with a little yard behind, which we paved over, with flower-beds in two corners. We moved there later in the year. In the summer Hugh Walpole, who was working in Hollywood, lent us Brackenburn for a fortnight, with that nice couple,

Jack and Edith, to look after us, any amount of food and drink, a superb library, and a rowing-boat on the lake.

One lovely hot sunny morning I rowed us almost the whole length of the lake – a good two miles – to Keswick at its northern extremity. There we happily shopped and explored, but by the time we were half-way home I felt so hot and exhausted that I took off my clothes, jumped into the water and had a most refreshing swim. Then I found that my arms, weakened by so much unaccustomed rowing, weren't strong enough to haul me back into the boat. After several failures I gave up, and poor pregnant little Comfort had to row us home with a large naked body hanging on to the stern of the boat.

[21]

When we had settled at Lloyd Square we found a living-in man and wife to run the house and, on Deirdre's recommendation, booked the services of Sister Cooper for January. She was an accomplished midwife and monthly nurse who became one of the family.

On New Year's Day 1935 I began to write some daily notes.

1 January. Kate O'Brien and Mary O'Neill to supper. Very affect-ionate and appreciative. Pleasant evening full of laughter. Comfort sobbed bitterly in her sleep, dreaming that she had lost me.

9 January. E. G. very interesting about Doughty. In 1888 Mac-millan said they would publish *Arabia Deserta* if it was rewritten from beginning to end by someone who knew English.

10 January. C. had indications of approaching baby, so called Sister Cooper from Salisbury.

11 January. Little progress by 6 p.m., so took C. and Sister C. to the Blue Hall cinema at the Angel. Saw an amusing film called *Hide-Out* with Robert Montgomery in it, also a full hour of very bad variety. Happily the baby began to make itself felt.

12 January. C. slept very little. Very uncomfortable all day, pains gradually increasing in violence. Her mother arrived at 4.30 p.m. and after a time C. whispered that I *must* get rid of her, so at 7 I persuaded her to go to a cinema to fill in time. She obediently drove off in her little car, and when she got to Bedford Square she was hit broadside on by another car and turned upside down. Miraculously she was only shocked, but she didn't come back that night.

Dr Hughes came at 9, put C. to bed and gave her chloral. She slept from 9.45 till 10.30, then woke with fearful pain. Sat with her till Dr Hughes came back just before 1 a.m. He had been called out from a late-night party and arrived in white tie and tails, which he quickly covered with a surgeon's white coat. Then I sat alone downstairs for an hour and a half, until

13 January. (The day the Saar Valley voted itself back to Germany) At 2.20 a.m. Bridget was safely born. She looked perfectly hideous, with a huge mouth, black and swollen head, a lot of fluffy hair and heavy red eyelids. She weighed 6 lb 10 oz. All spent rest of day in happy coma. In it I started reading the first volume of Sacha Guitry's *Souvenirs*, in which he described his own birth:

> *Lorsque je vins au monde j'étais extrêmement rouge. Mes parents me regardèrent avec effroi, puis ils se regardèrent avec tristesse, et mon père dit à ma mère: 'C'est un monstre, mais ça ne fait rien, nous l'aimerons bien tout de même.'*

I showed this to Comfort and we decided to follow the words of that delightful actor's parents.

Dr Glyn Hughes was a splendid fellow, large and good-looking, a former rugger-player. In the Great War he won an M.C., two D.S.O.s and the Croix de Guerre, and in the Second War, in which he won a third D.S.O., he ended as a Brigadier, Deputy Director of Medical Services in the Army. Just the man to have beside one in a crisis.

15 January. Registered Bridget's birth at Finsbury Town Hall. When it came to 'wife's Christian name', I said jovially: 'we have some funny names in our family. She's called Comfort'. 'Funny name?' said the outraged registrar, 'it's *my* name.' And sure enough he was called Mr Comfort. I soothed him down as best I could.

17 January. Photographed Bridget on balcony, and she enjoyed it. Early sign of vanity?

[22]

7 March. Lunched with John Collier at the Café Royal and returned to Bedford Square to find Bob closeted with T. E. Lawrence (or, as he now calls himself, Shaw), who had recently retired from the R.A.F. and was on the way to his home in Dorset. I joined them and we talked for an hour and a half. Liked T. E. enormously.

We spoke much of music and his gramophone. He prefers the music of strings to all other. 'A quartet is nearly perfect, a quintet is perfection.' Showed huge technical grasp of various subjects. Is keeping away from Wool and his cottage for the moment as the place is full of journalists, looking for him. I asked him how long he would like to live. He said 'Always one year less than I already have'. Seemed delighted with the joke of our having, technically, 'turned down' *The Mint*, his book about the Air Force, on which we had an option. He demanded a million pounds advance and 75 per cent royalty, thus effectively showing the fallibility of option clauses.[1] He was young and gay and friendly, tilting back his chair like a boy. He walked quietly away, without hat or coat. I felt, for the only time in my life, that I could have followed him anywhere. He was killed in a motor-cycle accident on 19 May.

[1] Cape eventually published *The Mint* in 1955.

[23]

Within the next few months Bridget turned into a pretty little girl, with fair hair and engaging features. In June we took her to stay with the Linklaters in Orkney. For the twelve train-hours to Aberdeen we put her in her basket on the luggage-rack in our carriage, where she slept uninterruptedly. In the twelve-hour sea-journey to Kirkwall Comfort fed her and then she sat calmly between us at the Captain's table for lunch.

Bridget in Orkney, June 1935

The excitement at Cape's in those days was the imminent publication of the first unexpurgated edition of *Seven Pillars of Wisdom*. Hamish and I had spent weeks adapting the page-headings of the old privately printed edition, and where necessary inventing new ones. The first bound copy reached the office while I was in Orkney, and Bob sent it to me, well wrapped up, to see whether the dust-jacket was strong enough for the large heavy book. I telegraphed to say it had arrived intact, and it wasn't until two or more copies were in the same parcel that the weight of the books split the dust-jackets nearly down the spine, and the whole edition had to be rejacketed in stronger paper. The reviews were stupendous, including a glowing one by Winston Churchill, the sales were phenomenal, and Cape's annual turnover was double their previous highest, and so it stayed thereafter. That year Cape and Howard shared a bonus of £10,000. I was given one of £400.

Meanwhile far away in February Peter Fleming had begun his marathon journey from Peking to Kashmir in North India – 3500 miles, which he covered on horseback and on foot in seven months, accompanied by the Swiss traveller and mountaineer Ella (Kini) Maillart. He later described the journey in *News from Tartary*. In the few letters he managed to send Celia he concealed the fact that he was travelling alone with another girl, and on the eve of his return in September he sent me a cable, including the words: 'Debag Swiss cat if Celia coming Croydon'. Luckily she didn't come to the airport and he was met there by his mother and me.

[24]

Late in 1935 I suddenly discovered that no work of the great American poet Robert Frost was available in England, where his first two books had appeared after being rejected by most American publishers. So I wrote to him, suggesting that he should make a selection of his poems, and I would get four leading poets to write introductory pieces, the book to be published by Cape. Frost agreed, the introductions were written by W. H. Auden, Cecil Day Lewis, Edwin Muir and the American poet Paul Engle, and the book was published by Cape in 1936. The five letters I received from Frost are here reproduced as Appendix B on pp. 183–187. I met him only once, in 1957, when in his early eighties he came over to receive doctorates from Oxford and Cambridge. In my copy of *Selected Poems* he wrote: 'To Rupert Hart-Davis, my rediscoverer, Robert Frost gratefully. London, May 28,

1957'. He was a fine poet and, as may be seen in his letters, a darlin' man.

Cape had been almost the first English publisher to visit the United States in search of books and authors: hitherto the traffic had been mostly in the opposite direction, and very soon he had signed up three future Nobel Prizewinners – Sinclair Lewis, Ernest Hemingway and Eugene O'Neill. Now he said it was my turn to make myself known to American publishers, and as I was going to stay with relations he agreed to pay for Comfort's passage as well as mine. So, after attending Peter and Celia's wedding in Chelsea Old Church on 10 December, a week later, in a thick fog, we tearfully left Bridget jumping gaily up and down in her cot, in the charge of the admirable Nurse Brooks, who sent us weekly radiograms reporting on her progress. Later in the day we embarked at Southampton on R.M.S. *Majestic* and prepared for my first Atlantic crossing.

[25]

Comfort was again pregnant, but she stood the crossing well. The first sight of New York from the sea is magical, and I was overwhelmed by its beauty. We stayed with Comfort's Aunt Joyce, the only one of the Borden family who for some reason had not lost her money in the Wall Street Crash, so she was still very rich. She was married to a second-rate Croatian fiddler called Zlatko Balokovic. He talked a great deal, and his favourite mode of conversation was to ask you what you did, and then tell you at length how to do it. Later I derived much secret amusement from hearing him, who had in the war been a private soldier on the other side, lecturing General Spears on military tactics and strategy. In his flow of talk he frequently used the word 'persemple', which I imagine was an anglicisation of the French *par exemple*. He and Joyce lived in a large and beautifully furnished New York apartment, with a butler and a number of other servants. One room contained nothing but an air-conditioner, a spray of water, and a Stradivarius violin, which Joyce had bought for him.

After celebrating Christmas and New Year with them we spent two days in Boston, visiting the publishers there, and two in Toronto to meet Cape's Canadian agents. When we arrived at what was, no doubt rightly, called The Largest Hotel in the British Empire, I was starting a cold in the head, so rang for room service and asked for a large whisky. I was told that, for some reason, no alcohol could be served

Toronto 1936

that day. My annoyance was magnified by the noise down the corridor of popping corks and roistering voices, coming, I was told, from a Convention of Boot-and-Shoe Operatives, who had presumably brought their liquor with them.

Next day we were guests at a large luncheon-party, and I was interviewed and photographed, but the noise of railway trains apparently under the hotel, and the sight of the flat grey immensity of Lake Ontario, added to my cold and made us thankful to return to the fleshpots of New York.

The friendliness and hospitality of the publishers there were almost overpowering. I visited more than a dozen of them during the next week, and the ones I liked best were Alfred Knopf, Ben Huebsch of the Viking Press, and Cass Canfield of Harper's. On 22 January 1936 we sailed for home feeling both exhilarated and exhausted.

[26]

When I was working for Heinemann my uncle Duff was hard at work on his first book, a life of Talleyrand. He gave me a typescript of the first few chapters, which I proudly showed to Charley Evans, who said he was too busy to read them and passed them on to Frere, who passed them back to me, saying they were no good. Now I was able to show the complete work to Jonathan, who published it with huge success, edition after edition. I also advised him to take over the books of William Plomer, whom I had met with Hugh Walpole and liked very much, and to pay Cecil Day Lewis £300 a year for three years for three straight novels, so as to release him from schoolmastering. Both William and Cecil stayed with Cape thereafter.

William Plomer

Other authors whom I brought to Cape included the best-ever writer about cricket, Neville Cardus. After the war I compiled a volume of his writings, which Cape published as *The Essential Neville Cardus*. In my copy he wrote 'To the Essential Rupert from the Quintessential Neville'.

Even better company was Johnny Morton, whose Beachcomber column had been the mainstay of the *Daily Express* for many years. He was a small jolly-looking man, always gay and amusing. One day we were lunching at Simpson's in the Strand. When our waiter passed our

With Beachcomber chez lui

table Johnny called out: 'Waiter, may I have some bread?' No response. The waiter passed again: 'Waiter, may I put my name down for some bread?' And at a third passing: 'Waiter, may I put my son's name down for some bread?' But he went breadless.

I took Johnny to one of the firm's weekly lunches at the Etoile, and introduced him to E. G. as Beachcomber. The old man had probably never seen the *Daily Express*, took my introduction to mean a real beachcomber, and immediately, in all sincerity, began questioning Johnny about which beaches he had combed. Johnny played up beautifully, describing the Gilbert and Ellice Islands and others in the Pacific Ocean, which neither of them had ever seen, until the conversation became general. Cape published several of Johnny's books.

[27]

At 3.15 p.m. on 3 June 1936 our son Duff was born in Lloyd Square, attended by Dr Hughes and Sister Cooper. It was a much easier birth than Bridget's, and he looked the right shape and colour. We spent our summer holiday in a farmhouse near the sea in Hampshire. Each morning I took Bridget down to the windswept beach, where I sheltered behind a breakwater while she staggered happily about with her little spade and bucket. Comfort stayed in the farm with the infant Duff.

*Nanny Barker and children
at Stormont Road*

Two small children were going to be difficult for Comfort to handle, so, once again on Deirdre's recommendation, we engaged Nanny Barker, who had a wonderful gift of soothing and loving babies. She stayed with us as long as she could, and in later years came back to look after Duff's children – a lifelong and much loved family friend.

We had enjoyed the house in Lloyd Square, but once again we decided that we ought to move. There was a little garden in the middle of the square, which was owned and looked after by nuns from the nearby convent, but they were naturally unwilling to allow small chidren to run about in it, and there was no park within walking distance. We therefore drove in our little Morris two-seater to all the London parks, and agreed that Ken Wood was much the nicest.

Estate agents produced a decent house very near the entrance to the park, but it was for sale, not rent. So I applied to my father. My mother's mother, who died in January 1925, left £11,000 to my mother in her will, but this had to go through the tedious processes of Scottish law, and when my mother died in January 1927 she had received nothing, and had made no will, so when the money eventually arrived it went to her next-of-kin, my father. We all knew that if the money had reached her she would have left it to Deirdre and me, but my father refused to part with it. Now, when for the first time I needed a lump sum, I asked him for £2000, which he reluctantly gave me.

I borrowed another £2000 from Jonathan, the sale went through on 13 January 1937, and for the first time, I had a house of my own, 32

Hugh Walpole at Stormont Road with his biographer and Comfort

Stormont Road, a turning off Hampstead Lane. It was a relatively modern house, comfortable and convenient, with a garage, a tiny garden in front and a large one at the back, in the far corner of which we made a sand-pit, which the children greatly enjoyed.

During the 1930s the *Sunday Times* held an annual Book Exhibition in Dorland Hall, Lower Regent Street. All the leading publishers took stalls at £30 apiece, on which they displayed their latest and most successful books. The exhibition lasted for a fortnight, on each day of which there were three lectures in the afternoon and evening. In 1936 I was cajoled into finding thirty-five speakers, with a chairman each, to perform from November 3 to 16. This took many weeks to arrange, but I had more acceptances than refusals, and the final list of speakers seems to me very creditable (see overleaf).

Much the most amusing lecture was that given by the immensely popular king of yachtsmen Uffa Fox. He was some way from sober when he arrived, and I noticed the top of a small whisky-bottle in his

SPEAKERS AT THE "SUNDAY TIMES" BOOK EXHIBITION

Dorland Hall, Lower Regent Street, S.W.1, November 2nd to 16th, 1936

Monday, Nov. 2nd, 3.30: Opening by the Lord Chief Justice (Lord Hewart of Bury)

Tuesday 3rd		4.30: A. E. W. Mason "The Historical Novel." *Chairman:* W. W. Hadley	6.15: Cecil Roberts , "Living and Writing." *Chairman:* Hon. Denis Berry
Wednesday 4th	2.30: Lord Dunsany "The Recent Change in the Language." *Chairman:* R. Ellis Roberts	4.30: Georges Duhamel *Mary Borden* "The Literary Entente Cordiale." *Chairman:* Brig.-Gen. E. L. Spears, *AN. OTHER MP.*	6.15: Christopher Stone "The Recording of Things." *Chairman:* Eric Maschwitz
Thursday 5th	2.30: Aldous Huxley Readings from his works. *Chairman:* Rose Macaulay	4.30: Ann Bridge "Accuracy in Fiction." *Chairman:* John Brophy	6.15: Peter Fleming "Travelling Light." *Chairman:* Lord Birkenhead
Friday 6th	2.30: Dr. Halliday Sutherland "Dogs in Literature." *Chairman:* Richard O'Sullivan, K.C.	4.30: L. A. G. Strong "Writing as a Career." *Chairman:* Richard Church	6.15: Uffa Fox "Sailing." *Chairman:* F. G. Mitchell
Saturday 7th	2.30: Alec Waugh "A Story-teller's Workshop." *Chairman:* Ralph Straus	4.30: Air-Comm. L. E. O. Charlton "War Over England, Then and Now." *Chairman:* Capt. H. A. Jones	6.15: Sydney Carroll "Can Stars Make Plays?" *Chairman:* Lilian Braithwaite

---

Nov. 9th, 2.15: Opening by the Rt. Hon. Oliver Stanley, President of the Board of Education.

Monday 9th	2.45: Dr. W. H. Hay "The Commonsense of Correct Eating." *Chairman:* Reginald Simpson	4.30: Dame Ethel Smyth "Dogs." *Chairman:* Christopher St. John	6.15: C. S. Forester "Marionettes." *Chairman:* George W. Bishop
Tuesday 10th	2.30: Walter Starkie "Minstrel in Spain." *Chairman:* Arthur Rackham	4.30: X. M. Boulestin "Cookery Books." *Chairman:* James Laver	6.15: Rom Landau "The Secrets of 'Seven.'" *Chairman:* F. Yeats-Brown
Wednesday 11th	2.30: J. E. Neale "Some Elizabethan Mysteries." *Chairman:* Sir Denison Ross	4.30: Admiral Sir Roger Keyes, Bt. "The Lessons of Naval History." *Chairman:* Sir Herbert Morgan	6.15: A. G. Street "Our Vanishing Countryside." *Chairman:* Clough Williams-Ellis
Thursday 12th	2.30: Margaret Irwin "Why Do You Do It?" *Chairman:* Eiluned Lewis	4.30. D. R. Jardine "Cricketing Facts and Fictions." *Chairman:* Howard Marshall	6.15: Rt. Hon. Duff Cooper M.P. "Biography." *Chairman:* Lady Birkenhead
Friday 13th	2.30: Bernard Darwin "Writing About Golf." *Cyril* *Chairman:* Moray Maclaren *Lakin*	4.30: Dorothy L. Sayers "The Technique of Murder." *Chairman:* Milward Kennedy	6.15: Eric Linklater "The Happy Author." *Chairman:* Elizabeth Haldane, C.H.
Saturday 14th	2.30: Stephen Spender "Modern Poetry." *Chairman:* Herbert Read	4.30: E. M. Delafield "Children's Books." *Chairman:* Hon. Mrs. St. Aubyn	6.15: J. B. Priestley "The Author and the Modern World." *Chairman:* Sylvia Lynd
Monday 16th	2.30: Graham Greene "A Novelist's Belief." *Chairman:* Douglas Woodruff	4.30: Helen Simpson "English Literature Transplanted." *Chairman:* J. G. Wilson	6.15: Philip Guedalla Closing Lecture. *Chairman:* Hon. Seymour Berry

The new documentary film about Books, "Cover to Cover," will be shown every day while the Exhibition is open, at 12.30, 3.30, and 7.

jacket pocket. However he started confidently at 6.15 p.m., but at about 6.20 p.m. every light in the building went out. It took me a long time to find an electrician, but Uffa went steadily on with his talk. He had clearly given it a hundred times before and knew it by heart, so darkness was no handicap. But it didn't help the projectionist who was supposed to be showing Uffa's slides on a screen behind him. The cues for slides were part of what the speaker knew by heart, and every time he came to one he said 'Slide Three' or whichever, probably had a nip of whisky, and then continued his talk. I imagine the half-bottle was empty by the time the lights came on, but the packed audience had thoroughly enjoyed the whole sterling performance.

[28]

On 19 February 1937 dear old Edward Garnett suddenly died. I went sorrowfully to his funeral at Golders Green, along with Hamish Miles, H. E. Bates and other young writers who had known, loved and been helped by the old hero.

I urged Jonathan to employ William Plomer as reader in E. G.'s place. He hesitated for weeks, but in April he agreed to give William a six-months' trial at a salary of £25 a month. As William's biographer wrote: 'The association begun in this tentative way lasted for thirty-six years.' William never liked Jonathan much, but he respected him, much as E. G. had, and there was never a cross word between them. William often tried to avoid having a 'talk' with Jonathan, which consisted of an endless monologue, in which one subject led to another. William described this as 'monologue-rolling'.

After the weekly lunch I usually spent some time in the boardroom with William while he was going through the week's manuscripts, and I clearly remember the September afternoon when the pile contained two battered notebooks filled with old-fashioned spiky handwriting, and a note saying that they were part of the diary of a Victorian clergyman, the Rev. Robert Francis Kilvert, of which twenty-two volumes had survived. William struggled with a few pages of the handwriting and said: 'Oh Lord, I suppose I'd better take this away and have a look at it.' A week later he arrived saying: 'I think it's marvellous. Send for the other twenty volumes.' At the weekly lunch he persuaded Jonathan to publish a selected version, edited by himself, and Jonathan had the sense or flair to agree. William set aside all his own work and concentrated on the Kilvert diary, three substantial volumes of which were published in 1938, 1939 and 1940. They were greeted with the highest praise and compared with the diaries of Pepys and Evelyn. They sold for many years, and in 1944 William produced a slim volume of the most interesting entries in the diaries, which sold even better.

During these years my own book-collecting galloped ahead. In the years 1937–39 I acquired 740 books, which cost just over two shillings apiece. To earn a little extra money I reviewed plays and books for the *Spectator* from 1934 to 1940. I also compiled two General Knowledge papers for *The Times*.

I organised and captained a cricket eleven, composed of members of the firm and an occasional author. We played at week-ends against villages. At Little Chart, near Ashford in Kent, where H. E. Bates lived, it was impossible to prevent cows from invading the outfield, and we agreed that to hit a cow full toss would score six, and a hit after the ball bounced four. I kept wicket, and when one of the villagers jumped half-way down the pitch to attempt a tremendous slog, missed the ball, I stumped him when he was a good six feet out of his crease. 'How's THAT?' I cried exultantly. The square-leg umpire, who hadn't been attending, said: 'If you're going to start stumping people you'll have to warn me. Not out.' At David Garnett's village, Hilton in Huntingdonshire, he and I played out a long and very lucky last-wicket stand. At Oxford, where we played against our chief printers, the Alden Press, I proudly opened the innings with Edmund Blunden. He always refused to wear batting-gloves and often returned to the pavilion with blood-boltered hands. Peter Fleming, who was also in our side, said that every time a no-ball was bowled, the umpire called 'Misprint'.

For our summer holiday in 1937 we shared a delightful house in North Wales with Deirdre, Ronnie and their children Susie and Annabel. The house, called Borthwen, was near Portmeirion, and below it was an estuary with sandy beaches, on which the children happily played under the watchful eye of Nanny Barker.

Early in 1938 Hamish's place was taken by his friend Guy Chapman. Cape had published his life of William Beckford in 1937, and in my copy Guy wrote:

> To Rupert
> Who, through laborious days and
> nights, expelled the worst errors
> of spelling, grammar and syntax

Watching cricket at Hilton
(left to right) Celia, Peter Fleming, Derek Verschoyle, RHD and David Garnett

Opening the Innings with Edmund Blunden   *With David Garnett at Hilton*

Borthwen 1937

Guy Chapman

from this book, and would, but
for the dull insensibility of
the author, have completely
re-written it.

In hoc signo vinces

GUY CHAPMAN

He had been twice decorated for gallantry in the war, and like
Edmund Blunden, though less compellingly, was haunted by those four
years for the rest of his life, and loved to quote: '*La guerre, mon vieux,
c'est notre jeunesse, ensevelie et secrète*'. He looked somewhat like a tough
military man, but in fact he was kindly, humorous and bookish, with
a passion for history. He was happily married to the novelist Storm
Jameson. Bonamy Dobrée said of him: 'He grumbles his way through
life with indomitable gaiety.' He and William Plomer got on very well
and Guy became one of my dearest friends.

[29]

Soon after that Peter Fleming's eccentric grandmother died. She had
made no will, so her late husband's large fortune went to Peter's Uncle
Phil, his two sisters, and Peter's mother. Peter and his three brothers
got nothing. Later in the year Uncle Phil, who had plenty of land and
houses of his own, generously gave the 2000-acre Nettlebed estate near
Henley-on-Thames to Peter. It contained an enormous Edwardian
mansion, with twelve bathrooms, in each of which, Peter said, the taps
produced a different kind of soup. He couldn't possibly live there, so
the house and garden were given to St Mary's Hospital, Paddington,
as a convalescent home, and Peter began to arrange the building of a
house of his own, which he called Merrimoles, in a beautiful part of
the estate, with woods behind, and in front a long sloping view over
fields, above which on a clear day Windsor Castle was visible. About
a mile away was Bromsden Farm. It was an active cattle-farm, but its
farmhouse was unoccupied, and Peter offered to let it to us for ninety
pounds a year. It was an isolated red-brick Victorian house, surrounded
by woods on three sides on a spur of the Chilterns. It contained five
bedrooms and three reception rooms, which we later turned into four
by converting the dairy into a library. We had one good look at the
house and garden and gratefully accepted his offer. The house remained
our main family base until 1985, when Duff gave up the lease.

Deirdre with her daughters Susie, and Annabel and (left to right) Lydie, Marie and Alice Ozanne

We immediately started to redecorate and furnish the house as cheaply as possible, without despoiling Stormont Road, and in the early summer of 1939 we stayed there for the first time, with the children and Nanny Barker. At the beginning of the year I had been laid up for some time with influenza and recuperated at Brighton. During that time I let my moustache grow: it was not generally popular, but it gave me a quasi-military look which was useful in the next few years.

Deirdre and Ronnie had bought a spacious house at West Chiltington in Sussex, with a large garden through which a little stream flowed. We took the children there for a visit, and Duff was photographed holding his first cricket-bat.

When war was declared on 3 September we decided that Comfort, the children and Nanny should stay at Bromsden, while I stayed at Stormont Road during the week. That winter of the phoney war, when the blackout made travel difficult, I housed an unusual trio in Highgate – Ruth Atkinson, Guy Chapman and Charlie Marford. We all got on extremely well together, and Charlie was a joy to us all.

[30]

At the beginning of 1940 I wrote ten pages of a diary, covering January and February, from which I quote:

1 January. Left Bromsden 7.30. Breakfasted Merrimoles. Drove Peter to London through fog, snow and ice. At one went with Ruth Atkinson to National Gallery. Kenneth Clark conducted Haydn's *Toy Symphony*, nine pianists played Schumann's *Carnaval* in rotation – and other amusing stunts. Guy returned to Stormont Road. Reading *Dombey and Son*.

2 January. Lunched with Edmund and his Japanese friend Aki Hayashi at the Metropolitan in Farringdon Road. E was well and cheerful, though fed up with his parents-in-law, who have been evacuated to his flat in Oxford. Mrs N, he says, is always complaining that he isn't a gentleman. 'I know I'm not,' he tells her, 'And if it's a question of who married who, there's no doubt S married me, and not vice versa.' Which quells the old trout momentarily. Nevertheless, E is moving back into College next term. Hayashi got very flushed and giggly after a glass of sherry.

8 January. Good drive up. No frost or ice for first time in a week. Arthur Calder-Marshall called. Said he and Gollancz had left the Communist Party and become old-fashioned Liberals.

15 January. Left Bromsden 7.50 a.m. with C and Duffy. Hard frost, radiator boiled four times, ran out of petrol, persuaded garage-proprietor to sell me an uncoupled gallon. Eventually reached Stormont Road 10.45. Dr Ive came at noon and examined D skilfully. Diagnosed something wrong with the hip-joint, and arranged X-ray for 2 p.m. D justifiably scared of X-ray parlour, which looked like a well-equipped torture-chamber. Put C and D on 3.20 for Henley. All very tiring and worrying. D very sweet and good. Reading detective stories for *Spectator*.

16 January. Dr Ive telephoned to say X-rays show abnormal condition of both Duffy's hip-bones. He is to see a specialist next week.

17 January. Dined at National Liberal Club with Neville Cardus, who on Sunday is to fly to Australia. He was gay and excited about the journey, his first flight. In fourteen days, he said, he would be in midsummer, carried there on a magic carpet. If the aeroplane crashed, his epitaph should be 'Not Icarus but Icardus'.[1]

[1] In Greek legend Icarus managed to fly with waxed wings, but he flew too near the sun, the wax melted and he perished in the Aegean Sea.

24 January. Met C and Duffy at Paddington, and drove them to house of Eric Lloyd, orthopaedic specialist. He examined D and said he was 70 per cent certain he had tubercular hip, probably bilateral. Wouldn't commit himself as to certainty of cure, but said it would mean months in hospital in any case. Lunched at Stormont, then down to Great Ormond Street Hospital, where Mantoux and Sedimentation Tests were taken. Poor Duffy was scared stiff, and no wonder. Saw them off at Paddington 3.20.

26 January. Met C and Duffy again, and took them to Great Ormond Street. Both tests positive. Lunched Stormont, and all (with Charlie Marford) caught 3.20 to Henley. Desperately tired and worried, trying to work out ways and means.

27 January. Peter walked over from Merrimoles, and offered to forgo a year's rent of the farm, to help us pay for Duffy's hospital fees. Deep snow.

30 January. C came up, lunched together at Bertorelli's, visited Lloyd and Ive, discussed plans for getting Duffy into Wingfield Hospital at Headington, Oxford. Bob Howard gave me a cheque for £50 as an indefinite loan.

31 January. To Oxford 9.45. Met C at the Mitre and lunched there. By bus to Wingfield Hospital, where we saw Prof. Seddon and discussed taking Duffy there. Put C on 5 p.m. bus for Bix (our nearest village). My train over an hour late in starting. Home by 10 p.m. Guy made me some rum punch.

1 February. Spears rang up and said he was sending cheque for £25. Peter sent a coupon for five gallons of petrol.

6 February. In bed with sore throat.

7 February. Got up, still with sore throat, drove to the farm, lunched there, drove C and D to the Wingfield Hospital, Headington, then back to Highgate and bed 6 p.m.

8 February. In bed. Sent for Doctor Ive, who gave me some prontosil, the new wonder-drug.

10 February. Got up and drove Charlie to the farm, nine inches of flood-water in main street of Maidenhead, then on to Oxford. Lunched with C at the George grill, then did Duffy's jigsaw with him out of doors in arctic weather. He said 'When you come one day, how many days will you stay?' Had to tell him that I was leaving after tea, which I did, driving back to the farm. C is wonderfully competent and sensible.

11 February. Peaceful day with Charlie.

12 February.   Drove up early, leaving Charlie in sole possession of the farm. Plenty of arrears at the office.

13 February.   Sydney Cockerell brought in the typescript of a collection of letters received by him and edited by Viola Meynell – looks interesting.[1] S.C. very agreeable – a professional charmer. Jonathan is getting old, muddled and even more repetitive.

17 February.   To Oxford by bus on ice-slippery roads. Did new jigsaw with Duffy. Tea and anchovy toast in hospital canteen. Back to farm by bus. Peaceful evening with Charlie.

18 February.   Lazy snowbound day. In the middle of eating a sausage at breakfast, Bridget suddenly said to me: 'One day I had more treacle than porridge'.

19 February.   Back to London with Peter and Celia. Lunched with John Carter at the Bedford Head. At 9.30 p.m. Comfort rang up from Oxford to say that the doctors have agreed to our taking Duffy back to the farm on Saturday. (They had tried traction with no result.) Too excited to concentrate properly on a review for the *Spectator*.

21 February.   Telephoned C at mid-day and confirmed the arrangements for taking Duffy home. Lunched with William and Guy. Dined Etoile with Biblio Boys – John Carter, Michael Sadleir, Simon Nowell-Smith, Dudley Massey. On to Sadleir's flat and bourbon whisky. Home 12.30.

23 February.   Got home at 6.30 feeling feverish and ill, to find an urgent call from Comfort. Rang her up and found that the doctors had attempted to rescind their decision and now suggested an immediate exploratory operation as an attempt at a more definite diagnosis. Determined to prevent this, feeling sure that, while it might be interesting for the doctors, it would do nothing for the child. Rang up Eric Lloyd to get his advice – which was helpful. Rang C again and went to sleep after taking kaylene, bread-and-milk, and veganin.

24 February.   Much better after long heavy sleep. Drove down to the farm, where C telephoned to say hurry to Oxford to see doctors. Drove furiously to Headington, where we were kept waiting three-quarters of an hour. Then saw Doctor Foley and arranged to take D straight home, bringing him back in a fortnight for further examination and X-ray. Packed up everything and drove C and

---

[1] *The Best of Friends*, published by Cape in 1940

D back to the farm. D very gay and excited. When we drew near
and saw Nanny and Bridget waving to us, he could hardly contain
himself and said: 'This *is* fun'. Later both children got out of hand
with over-excitement and bawled continuously. Since Duff's pain
occurs only when he walks, we are keeping him sitting down,
mostly outside in a pram, where he saws wood and is happy.

25 February.   Lovely peaceful warm sunny day. Carted leaves and
manure to make hot-bed in the frame, finished reading Vol 17 of
Les Hommes de Bonne Volonté (by Jules Romains). Sawed some wood
with Charlie.

[31]

After the miracle of Dunkirk in May-June, and the start of the Battle
of Britain, fears of a German invasion grew. I joined the Local Defence
Volunteers (later called the Home Guard) at Bix. We drilled, fired
rifles, erected several useless road-blocks and set up a dawn-watch on
a little hill. One morning as darkness dispersed my colleague and I saw
what we thought was a fleet of falling parachutes. Luckily we deferred
reporting the danger until the growing light showed us that we were
looking at the balloon-barrage over Slough.

By now the Government was urging all women and children who had
relations in America to go there, and Comfort's Aunt Joyce wrote
begging me to send them over to the house in Camden on the coast of
Maine, where she and Zlatko were now living, near Comfort's sister
Emmy and her American husband and children. After much agonised
discussion we decided they had better go, and I booked passages for
them in July.

Getting visas was difficult. There was a long queue round the government office where British ones were issued, but I discovered that the
granting of visas depended only on where you were born. Comfort was
born in India, and, armed with her birth-certificate, we went to the
India Office, where there was no queue and we got the visas immediately. So these three little blonde creatures entered the United States
of America as three Indians.

When the sad time came we all four travelled to Liverpool on 9 July,
spent a sleepless night in the Adelphi Hotel, and next afternoon went
down to the Mersey. As so often happens in such places, we had to
walk a good hundred yards down a concrete path, show passes, tickets
and visas at the end, then walk another hundred yards back on the

other side. I had to carry Duff all the way: he was a hefty four-year-old and I held him first in one arm, then in the other. When we were waiting for the others at the foot of the gang-plank a benign old clergyman came up to us and said: 'Hallo, my little man, are you going all the way to America?' Duff, who was as exhausted as I was, didn't answer but drew back his right arm and hit the good cleric as hard as he could on the chest. He departed discomfited.

When we got on to the Cunard Line S.S. *Antonia* we found her already chock-full of women and children. Comfort was told that she must carry three lifebelts everywhere throughout the voyage. We had a miserable tea in the saloon and then I had to leave them in their tiny cabin. To fill an hour or two before the London train I went to a cinema, but saw and heard little of the film, in which Robert Montgomery was again the hero. I was sunk in misery, anxiety and loss.

PART THREE : THE ARMY

L'armée est une nation dans la Nation;
c'est un vice de nos temps.

ALFRED DE VIGNY

[1]

EXCEPT FOR a week's holiday later in the month I spent the rest of July commuting on week-days from Bromsden to the office, which was in a state of stagnation. The bookselling boom of the next few years had not begun. William had left for a job in the Admiralty, Guy had applied for a commission in the Army, and Ruth Atkinson had gone to a war job. Molly came to stay at Bromsden, where she was soon joined by Charlie. Between them they did a lot of gardening and other hard work, while Nanny cooked for us. On most week-end evenings I drove over to Merrimoles and played bridge with Celia and either Tim and Rosalie Nugent or Celia's parents. One evening her father, a darling old retired doctor, dropped all his cards on the floor. Celia said: 'Daddy, what *are* you doing?' He gave a sweet smile and said 'Conjuring'.

On 19 July a cable announced the safe arrival of my three little Indians at Quebec, whence Emmy's husband Ham (short for Hamilton) Hall drove them down to Camden. Next day Deirdre and her two children sailed for America, and I had to register for the Army with my age-group at the Henley Labour Exchange. They told me I would not be called up for some time.

One day, when Charlie and I were shopping in Henley, we came out of a tobacconist-cum-sweetshop which had a very pretty girl behind the counter, and Charlie said: 'I'll tell you something, boy. I'd rather be in her than in the Leicester Little Theatre Movement'.

On 31 July Nanny left tearfully, and I received my first letter from Comfort – twenty pages written during the voyage. I had posted one every day since she left. After that we both wrote regularly and almost all our letters have survived. Some arrived in a week, some in a month or more, so that a question took weeks to be answered. We therefore concentrated on telling each other exactly what we were doing every day, I describing every flower in the Bromsden garden. All the letters are full of love and longing for reunion. All mine were opened by the Censor, and most of Comfort's. Once, when I inadvertently said where one bomb had dropped, the Censor very neatly cut out the name of the place, so as not to spoil the rest of the letter.

Sunflowers at Bromsden

During my holiday I spent one night at Blockley and one with my Aunt Madge at Bath, the rest at Bromsden. Realising that when I was called up I might be conscripted anywhere in an unsuitable unit, I decided to see whether I could do better on my own by volunteering elsewhere, so on 1 August I travelled by train to Reading and presented myself at the recruiting office. For half-an-hour I was examined by six doctors, being passed on by one to another. I had so long considered myself a pot-bellied, desk-bound wage-slave that I was astonished and somewhat pleased when one doctor after another commented favourably on my physique. My chest-expansion was the best they'd had for days and so on. Eventually I was passed Grade One (the top) and was then interviewed by a friendly old dug-out colonel. Having read my *curriculum vitae* he said: 'I suppose you'd like to get a commission as soon as possible.' I said yes, and he advised me to volunteer for the Brigade of Guards, whose recruiting office was on the other side of the street. Clutching my medical certificate I took his advice. I was accepted at once for the Coldstream Guards and told to report to Reading again in a week's time.

Next day I lunched at White's Club with my and Peter's dear friend Tim Nugent, who was now Brigade Major of the whole Brigade. In the Great War he had won an M.C. with the Irish Guards, then became Comptroller of the Lord Chamberlain's Department and Equerry to the King. After lunch he rang up a bigwig in the Coldstream and told him about me. On 5 August I received a letter from Reading, saying that on second thoughts my eyesight wasn't good enough for the Guards and I needn't report to them again.

Next day I was summoned to an interview with the Regimental Adjutant of the Coldstream, who said they would accept me as a potential officer, in which case my eyesight wouldn't matter, since officers were allowed to wear spectacles. The next potential officers' squad would assemble on 20 September. This gave me ample time to tidy up everything at home and office. My salary had now risen to £900, and the others agreed to pay me half that while I was in the army. I rejoined the Bix L.D.V. who had already given me a farewell party. I also for the first time visited John and Myfanwy Piper at their home in Fawley Bottom. They were angelically kind and agreed to house as many of my books as possible in an empty room. They became very dear friends. There was, as yet, no library at Bromsden.

On 19 August, as instructed, I reported at the West Croydon recruiting office and officially enlisted in the Coldstream Guards after another medical examination (Grade One again) and swearing an oath in company with five other men. Then I was given one day's pay (two shillings) and one day's ration allowance (ditto). It all took five hours and would have been very tiresome if one of the other men hadn't been

*Guardsman
Recruit*

a charming schoolmaster called John Darwall-Smith. We got on very well and he drove us to the Guards Depot at Caterham in Surrey, where we were welcomed by an officer and given leave-passes till 20 September. So now I was a Guardsman Recruit on leave. When I got home I compared my two medical reports and found they varied greatly. My height, weight, chest-measurements and colour of eyes were all different.

[2]

Charlie and I had been alone together at the farm for a week, getting on famously, with Charlie doing all the cooking. Then Molly returned, and they spent a lot of time picking and bottling fruit. Being an enlisted soldier I had to leave the L.D.V. for the second time, after a second lot of farewells in various pubs. Comfort's letters were now beginning to arrive, to my great joy. There were air-raids on London most nights, but at the farm we heard nothing. The last week-end of August I spent happily with Cecil and Mary Day Lewis in their home at Musbury, near Axminster. We sat in the sun behind the barbed wire on the sea-front at Seaton and played cricket with their two boys on an old tennis-court. In the evenings Cecil played and sang.

There began to be heavy air-raids on Central London by day and night, and at the office we all spent a great deal of time in the basement. On 13 September things got so bad that we closed the office and sent the staff home. Two of the girls, who lived on the outskirts of London, hadn't slept properly for six days, so I drove them down to Bromsden and left them with Charlie while I drove on to Blockley for a peaceful week-end.

I was thrilled to hear from Comfort that the specialist in Boston, Mass, to whom she had taken Duff, had found that new X-rays compared with the Oxford ones showed a considerable improvement in the hips. In his opinion the whole trouble had been caused by some nutritional deficiency in the bones, which, if Duff drank plenty of milk and did a few simple exercises, would soon disappear, which is exactly what happened. I thanked goodness that I had refused that exploratory operation.

I arranged for my bank to pay rent, rates, insurance etc, and sent them a document that gave Charlie authority to sign cheques on my behalf for tradesmen and suchlike. One evening I drove over from the farm and dined with the Pipers. John Betjeman was there and we sang old popular songs and played amusing pen-and-paper games.

On my last evening one of the bridge-players at Merrimoles was a delightful American diplomat from the London Embassy called Walt Butterworth, who had rented one of Peter's cottages for week-ends. At midnight he and I went over there and had a long heart-to-heart talk over whisky-and-soda. He was most intelligent, sympathetic, reassuring and compassionate, and he boosted my morale immensely. I owe him a great debt, but I have never seen him since the war. That night

I wrote a long letter to Comfort, and before I went to sleep I leaned out of my bedroom window, enjoying the smell of flowers and the silence, and wondering when I should see my home again.

Next morning, 20 September, I said goodbye to Charlie, who stayed to look after the farm, and even got himself a job in Henley's tiny theatre, to which he travelled by bicycle. Celia drove me to the station and I handed over our car to her care. John Darwall-Smith picked me up at the office, we lunched together and reported to Caterham well before the 4 p.m. deadline.

[3]

My first impression inside the Guards Depot was of an immense square of asphalt, flanked by large barrack-blocks, one of which had received a direct hit from a bomb which killed several recruits. On a large tract of adjacent land a number of huts had recently been built to house the latest intake. They were connected by narrow concrete paths through deep mud. There were twenty-two potential officers in our hut, and except for John Darwall-Smith (28) and myself (33) they were all under twenty and fresh from public schools, mostly Eton. To them the Depot seemed only slightly more uncomfortable than their school and they treated it as a lark. For John and me, who had been making ourselves comfortable for years, the contrast was a good deal greater. Also living in the hut with us was a dozy guardsman called a Trained Soldier, who was supposed to tell us what to do: we learned little from him.

But we were lucky with the man in charge of our squad. Sergeant Bowman was tall and good-looking, very intelligent and with a splendid sense of humour. He was just the man to control with firm friendliness a group of high-spirited schoolboys. (He ended the war as a Captain in the Devon Regiment.) One icy morning when we were standing in a circle being taught the names of the parts of a Bren gun, he looked at me and said: 'Don't stand with your arms folded, Hart-Davis. You look like a company director.' 'I *am* a company director, Sergeant', said I, and he burst out laughing. Whenever there was a bugle-warning of a local air-raid, we had to set off at the double with full kit and rifle to a trench on the perimeter of the Depot.

It was five days before I found time to scribble a few pencil lines to Comfort:[1]

25 September. I am sitting astride my bed, using the pillow as a desk. The other twenty-one chaps are writing home, reading newspapers, (which are delivered to the hut: John and I are going to share *The Times*), cleaning boots, equipment, floor etc. I've just polished two fire-buckets. At 3.30 we're going to get our first bath, a shower, of which we have two a week. It's more than forty-eight hours since we had to get into our trench, which is a great relief.

The chief thing up to now is that I'm enjoying it all. It's much more amusing than sitting in Bedford Square with nothing to do, waiting for the siren. It's like undertaking a rough and improbable adventure with a lot of schoolboys – a nice change from coping with authors and dictating letters. I sleep like a log every night from ten to six, despite guns, bombs, and the roar of planes [from the fighter-base at nearby Kenley]. The grub is rough and starchy, but one's always ravenous and it seems delicious. There's beer in the canteen, and we've a wireless in the hut, now playing selections from Noel Coward.

We have to do a terrific lot of cleaning – boots, brass, webbing (with khaki blanco). Also we have to fold up all our blankets in a certain way, and every so often lay out all our kit for inspection. An idiotic amount of importance is attached to that sort of thing.

27 September. I didn't expect to get any time to write today, but we're in our trench (at 9.30 a.m.) and there's a helluva battle going on overhead. Masses of planes, roars and cracks of different guns. Some of the lads are very excited and keep claiming to see Germans falling in flames. It's an amazing sight – bright sunlight, blue sky, puff after puff of smoke from the anti-aircraft fire, planes wheeling and circling like aimless birds. It's now 9.45, and the battle, though continuing, is further away. I'm sitting on a little seat in the trench, John is next to me, and Sergeant Bowman is on the firestep watching out. He is a *charming* man and we all dote on him. Most of the lads are beginning to try and grow a moustache – the only aspect of military life in which I'm for the moment ahead of them.

29 September. There's pretty good pandemonium going on in this recreation room, but I'll try to give you an account of an ordinary day. We are woken by a bugle (reveille) at 6 a.m. It is dark and usually

---

[1] From this and all subsequent letters I have removed most of the endearments, messages to the children etc. Otherwise they are just as I wrote them.

cold. We dash into socks, shoes, pants, shirts, sweaters and trousers and hurry across to the wash-house, which is quite near. There are a lot of basins, usually hot water, and some mirrors, though it's too dark to see properly.

Then we dash back to the hut and make our beds, sweep the floor (red composition stuff) with a dry broom and dash off to breakfast at 6.45. Several hundred men eat together, twelve to a table. I've never seen people eat so much so quickly, and we're getting pretty good at it ourselves.

Dash back to the hut, wash all the floor with water (a tiresome business with so many beds), lay out more kit for inspection, put on our boots, gaiters and hats and rush out for first parade at 8 a.m. There are three parades each morning of fifty minutes each, with brief intervals.

During these the recruits stand easy while the instructor fires questions – mostly military ones – at them. The last question usually is:

'What's the Regimental motto?'

'*Nulli Secundus*, Sergeant.'

'What does that mean?'

'Second to None, Sergeant.'

The recruit who answered the last question 'Better than Nothing, Sergeant' was whisked off to the Guardroom.

The parades vary between drill, musketry and P.T. Occasionally instead of a parade we have a lecture on health, army life etc. The one on gas-warfare caused some amusement. It was given by another sergeant who had been on a gas course and had learned every word of the official document by heart. When he came to 'This serves as a prophylactic', one of the mischievous lads said 'What's that, sergeant?' 'Don't interrupt me,' said the sergeant. I don't think either of them knew what the word meant.

Lunch is at 12.20. Then there are two more parades. Tea at 5.15, and then comes 'shining parade'. We sit on our beds, cleaning boots, brasses and webbing, while Sergeant Bowman talks to us about the history of the regiment.

As I wrote twelve years later:

There was a delightfully partisan directness about these simplified history lessons, in which nothing existed unless it had an immediate bearing on the activities of the Regiment. For the Coldstream recruit the earth was without form until in 1650 General Monck mustered the Lord General's Regiment of Foot-guards for service in Cromwell's New

Model Army, and the march to London from Coldstream in Scotland gave the Regiment its name. In 1660 they paraded on Tower Hill, laid down their arms in the name of Cromwell and took them up in the name of Charles II.

Thereafter the centuries are dotted with isolated deeds and actions: 'Nothing much happened for the next ten years; then there were some riots in London, and of course the Regiment was called in to put them down.' So the sergeant's voice continues, parrot-wise, evening after evening, until even the dullest guardsman begins to have an inkling of the glories to which he is heir.

Then we're free, and John and I usually go to the canteen, where we have sausage-and-mash and onions, beer or cider and an apple. Usually there's a raid alarm around 8, when the lights everywhere are switched off and we stumble back to the hut, put a candle on a bucket between our beds and read or talk till 9 or 10, when we go gratefully to sleep.

On Wednesday and Saturday we finish at mid-day, and on Sunday we have nothing to do, unless we're unlucky enough to be roped in for church parade (I've escaped so far). There are only three categories of religion in the army – C of E, R.C. and *Minor* Religions, which means all Nonconformists, Jews, Buddhists, Hindus, Sikhs, Muslims etc etc. Early one morning I heard the loud voice of an N.C.O. shouting abuse, and asked the Trained Soldier what it was. 'The minor religions falling in', he said. Since there are no places of worship for them, the poor wretches are put to scrub out the gym and the Naafi. Perhaps there'll be some conversions to Christianity.

After three weeks we're allowed out of barracks for one or two evenings a week, but we're allowed to visit only Caterham and Purley, so I expect we won't do more than have a bath and a meal. There are several telephone-boxes in the camp and yesterday I rang up Merrimoles. Peter was there and I had a word with them both – nice to hear familiar voices.

2 October. We're all very gay and cheerful, despite coughs and colds, from which all are suffering. Mine has, I hope, just about passed its peak. Charlie sent me a huge box of apples and pears from the farm, and they're a big success. There is certainly something to be said for the life here. The brain is given a complete rest in cotton-wool, while the body is brought up to scratch. We still spend a considerable time each day in our trench, where I read *The Times* and do the crossword.

6 October. Last night we were dragged out of bed into the trenches from 11 p.m. to midnight. Luckily it was quite warm. Some of the lads are charming, and the atmosphere is gay and jolly. When we're in our zigzag trenches at night the bright flashes from the shell-bursts light up our tin hats and still figures, like a shot in a very good film.

The canteens at night have a certain charm. They are long white buildings with iron rafters, rather like customs-sheds at ports. There are tables and chairs at each end, and several perpetual queues at the bars down one side – one for beer and cider, one for tea, one for hot food, one for cleaning materials etc. Directly the first air-raid warning goes after dark, the lights go out and they carry on with a few candles. There's a piano at the far end, on which are constantly played 'Roll out the Barrel', 'Lily of Laguna', 'Begin the Beguine' and other favourites. There are maybe 200 or 300 troops, eating, drinking, talking and singing, mostly in tin hats. Quite a good sight.

Wherever one goes, even fifty yards to the W.C., one is compelled to carry over one's shoulder a heavy service gas-mask in its case, a tin hat and a rolled-up gas-cape – an infernal nuisance at meals I can tell you.

I daresay this abrupt change into a completely unintellectual life is 'a good thing', provided it doesn't last too long. Just now I feel prepared to do anything in the world, so long as I can be with you and the children – in peace. Guy writes that the office is ringed with bomb-craters. Charlie is okay at the farm.

9 October. I've had two letters of yours (of Sept 9 and 14) and I can't tell you how excited and happy their arrival has made me.

13 October. Suddenly on Thursday your three missing letters (Aug 31, Sept 1 and 2) arrived. So altogether I got *five* last week. On the same day we passed our Third Week Inspection (by the Adjutant of the Depot) with flying colours. The squad was even complimented! We had our turn-out inspected, did some drill on the barrack-square and were asked questions about regimental history and customs. We are to have further inspections at the end of our sixth, seventh and eighth weeks.

Last night (Saturday), for the first time, we were allowed out of barracks. The excitement was intense. After cleaning ourselves and everything in sight we got out at about 3 p.m., proceeded to Lower Caterham by taxi and on foot, did some shopping (I bought this writing-paper), and went on to the Surrey Hills Hotel, where we had tea and dinner. The only hitch was that the hot baths they had promised us failed to materialise, owing to boiler trouble. But it was nice to sit by the fire in a chair (there are none here) and not having to rush off every few minutes. Most of the lads drank champagne at dinner and got a little tipsy. I stuck to whisky. We got the last bus back, arriving here soon after eleven.

Everything proceeded normally, and we had completed half our eight-weeks' course, when on Wednesday, 16 October, I had a nasty setback.

[4]

20 October.   Dene Military Hospital, Caterham

Don't be alarmed by this address, dearest. It's only my knee, which I put out excruciatingly on Wednesday. The whole squad was, as they say, 'proceeding' back to the hut, after firing on the range. We had to jump over a trench, about five feet deep, with banked-up clay on either side. The footholds were bad, and as I landed I must have twisted my knee. Anyway it gave under me, with a moment's blinding agony, and I performed a complete backwards somersault, landing on my head at the bottom of the trench. Luckily I fell absolutely limp, probably unconscious, and didn't hurt myself any more. Even my spectacles, which I was wearing, were untouched.

Sergeant Bowman and some of the boys fished me out, and four of them carried me up to the Medical Officer on a stretcher. He bandaged my knee up tight, to see what that would do. For the rest of the day I was 'excused all duties' (which is mysteriously called 'Attend C') and hobbled about with a stick. Next morning I visited the M.O. again, and after one look at the knee (then about the size of a large melon) he sent me here in an ambulance.

The hospital is a little way outside the Depot. It is a smallish two-storey house, and was an infant school before the war. Everything is very comfortable and easy-going, and I'm enjoying it immensely. There are fourteen beds in the one ward, but only ten occupied. All the chaps are nice, and they're a much better cross-section of 'the ranks' than my twenty-one public school boys. Next to me are a gardener from Wantage and a navvy from Eastbourne.

At the other end of the ward is a superb cockney humorist, Guardsman J. C. Green (Greenie to his friends). He is a tall man with a face rather like that of W. C. Fields, the American comedian, whom he can imitate perfectly. When he arrived, tottering in a high fever and carrying all his kit, he was waylaid at the entrance by a diminutive corporal in the Royal Army Medical Corps, who fired questions at him: 'Name, Number, Regiment, Age, Religion, Home Address' etc. Greenie simply looked at him and said: 'Blimey, where's Snow White and the other six?' Luckily he was too ill to be charged with insubordination.

Every time the Sister, a terrifying woman with red tabs on her uniform, comes into the ward he hails her in his W. C. Fields voice: 'Ullo, my little chickadee'. She is not amused. The nurses, who are dull and overworked but kind, he calls 'My little plums'. When during lunch a nurse came in and said: 'Would you like some more meat, Green?' he answered: '*More* meat, nurse? I'm dead-beat wrestling with the bit I've got'. Next day he said: 'Ullo, ullo, lunch is late again. Someone 'as blundered. It's Balaclava all over again.' He quickly realised that I am the only patient who fully appreciates his jokes, and he shouts them to me down the length of the ward.

We have the wireless on a good deal, mostly jazz, and I have plenty of time for reading. I brought a few books with me, and an old trout comes round twice a week with a book-trolley. The grub is tolerable, though less good than the Depot's. We can send out for tobacco, chocolate, apples etc. The air-raid shelter is a good underground one, and during raids all the mobile patients crowd into it and sing songs. Greenie gives spirited renderings of 'Dinah' and other songs, with his own syncopation.[1]

When I'd been here a day the doctor strapped my knee up very tight with elastoplast. He said it was synovitis, which I imagine simply means fluid on the joint. The swelling has gone down a lot. I suppose I shall be in here about another week, which would suit me fine. I hope it isn't longer, because then I should run the risk of losing my place in the squad, which would be an infernal nuisance.

I can't remember whether I told you, but I eventually won the argument about the marriage allowance. I get paid seven shillings and sixpence a week at the Depot, and they pay twenty-seven shillings a week into your account at Highgate – at least I hope they do. I must write and find out whether it's coming in okay.

Who should turn up this morning but dear old Jamie. He was very gay and sweet, and I was delighted to see him. I've also had a visit from John Darwall-Smith. It's a lovely change not to do any drilling

---

[1] Four years later I arranged for Greenie and his brother to give a concert to the troops at Pirbright, which was a great success. After the war he brought his beautiful fiancée to see me in my office, and we corresponded with Christmas cards (his full of rude jokes) every year until he died in 1989.

or cleaning for a bit, and since I feel perfectly well I can get a great deal of enjoyment out of the comedies of hospital life.

22 October. Three lovely letters arrived yesterday, via farm and Depot. I almost shed a few tears when I had finished reading them. My knee is slowly mending, but the elastoplast makes it very stiff and unwieldy.

25 October. I've been here eight days now, and though my knee's much better, it isn't right yet, and I have a nasty idea that I may have to stay here another week, and it's looking more and more as though I shan't be back in time to pass out with the rest of the squad, in which case I shall have to start *all over again* with the next squad, which arrives late in November, and the four weeks I'd done before my accident will be wasted. And yet what does it really matter? The whole of the army is so idiotic that it's quite immaterial which part of it one's muddling about in. With any luck I should get a week or so's leave before the new squad assembles. What the hell! There are only two things now— good, which is reunion with you and the children – and bad, which is everything else.

I've had two delicious hot baths since I last wrote, the first since I left the farm. The navvy next to me has been replaced by a grave-digger from Northampton, a dull but friendly and honest fellow. He has told me all about his wife and child, and all about the digging of graves. The gardener on my other side has had a mass of parcels from home, mostly containing glacier mints, which he presses on me and I greedily accept. Someone is playing a piano very badly upstairs.

28 October. When the doctor came round this morning I asked him how much longer he thought I should have to stay here and he said a fortnight. This mucks up my last chance of catching my own squad, but I'm entirely fatalistic and philosophical about the whole business now, and only hope I get my seven days' leave. Now that I've stopped worrying about getting back in time, I feel quite cloddishly peaceful again. There's a pretty generally accepted theory that army tea is liberally dosed with some kind of *an*aphrodisiac bromide, to subdue the men's lusts and induce sleep. Whether that is the reason or not, I certainly experienced a complete mental and intellectual fatigue while I was there. To a certain extent the same inertia still exists: we have army tea here, there's no privacy at all, and the effing wireless never stops for a second, so you'll have to make allowances.

30 October. I'm up for the first time to-day, dressed in my wounded soldier clothes (blue coat and trousers, white shirt, red tie). My knee is tightly bandaged, and with occasional aches and twinges it will do very well for ordinary activities, but not for drilling or marching.

I'm deep in *The Old Wives' Tale*, which I'm thoroughly enjoying. I've hardly been smoking in bed, but to-day I've got my biggest pipe going full bat. General improvement in fact. The wireless has just been turned up very loud (a yodelling programme). Almost every evening we have to go out to the shelter from about 7.30 till 9. It's stifling in the ward at night, since the blackout boards seal up every crack. After a day or two I got quite used to it.

31 October.   They now say I'm to be sent to Redhill for an X-ray, and to Millbank (London) for a specialist's opinion.

2 November.   Two more lovely letters this morning (those of October 9 and 10), only two days after the last two: they bring you and the children so close to me. Greenie has left, and the chaps still in the ward are a clerk from Barrow-in-Furness, a tobacconist from Notting Hill Gate, a railway-shunter from Birmingham and a groundsman-cum-football-pro from Mansfield, Notts. At the moment they're all arguing with one of the nurses as to who had a bath last.

4 November.   Yesterday the Company Commander came to see me. He said I should definitely have to start all over again with another squad, probably around the end of this month. He also said he'd do what he could to arrange sick-leave in between.

I've at last managed to get *The Times* delivered daily, and happily do the crosswords, only they don't last long enough.

7 November.   Three weeks to-day I've been in here, and I don't mind telling you I'm fed up to the back teeth with it. It's over ten days since the doctor here (so he says) applied for an appointment at Millbank. Am now trying to bribe one of the nurses to *telephone* and find out what's happening, but it's uphill work.

I was going to write yesterday afternoon, but had two hours' deep sleep instead. Just as well I did, or else I should have been dragged off to bail out the air-raid shelter, which was full of water.

Yesterday morning we were woken by a stick of bombs, which fell very near with a terrific crash. We're all now expert at getting under our beds in record time. Sometimes I feel a bit nervous at night; indeed I don't know anyone who doesn't. The crash, roar, thud of guns and bombs, with the irregular drone of German engines, goes on for hours most nights. After lights-out I go to sleep with cotton-wool in my ears. Nothing actually shakes the house except a bomb exploding pretty close. I'm reading *The Moonstone* with pleasure.

9 November.   This morning I heard that I've an appointment with a specialist in London next Tuesday. Even in the army I feel this must lead to something. One of the nurses gave me a couple of postcards and I've sent them to the children. They're gradually getting the up-patients to do more and more of the work of the hospital, and there are mutterings all round. I and another lad had to wash up dozens of greasy plates yesterday. Luckily the water was hot, and we got an extra cup of tea for our pains. So little happens here that it's almost like a prisoner-of-war camp. A visitor on Sunday is an event, and the Saturday football-sweep is discussed for two whole days.

13 November. This is almost certainly the last letter I shall write you from this blue-pencil building. Yesterday I set off at 10.15 a.m., dressed once again in my khaki, and was driven very fast to London in the back of a huge and highly uncomfortable ambulance. There was one other chap in it, suffering from scabies, so I sat in the far corner and lit up my pipe.

We got to Millbank at 11.15, and then, needless to say, I had to wait $1\frac{3}{4}$ hours – not in a comparatively decent waiting-room, but standing up in a first-floor corridor, all windows down both sides, and not a pane of glass left. The cold was severe. I had taken some cheese sandwiches and chocolate from here, and at about 12 I ate them. Every now and then a fat officer in a tin hat (there was a warning on) padded past me. I held the grub behind me with my left hand and saluted him smartly with my right. After a bit I was joined by a chap who had broken his spine in two places and was waiting to be examined for his disability pension. He told me he had a steel support down his back, but he looked okay. Walking up and down the icy corridor (it was about 200 yards long) to prevent rigor mortis setting in, I spied a public telephone in a niche, and borrowing a penny from the broken-back I rang the office and had a crack with Guy.

Eventually I saw a very nice Canadian specialist called McDougall. He examined my knee and was most encouraging. Said the cartilage was not affected, but a ligament had suffered a severe sprain. He put on a new crêpe bandage and told me to keep it on until I feel I can do without it.

When I came down from seeing him there was no sign of my driver or ambulance, so I whipped round the corner and found a pub just behind the Westminster Ice Rink. There I consumed $1\frac{1}{2}$ pints of excellent beer (my first drink for four weeks), then nipped back, found my driver and was driven back here, alone this time and a little drowsy after the beer.

They're letting me out of here tomorrow afternoon, when I shall trek to the Depot and spend the night there. The hope is that on Friday they'll let me go home on sick-leave for a fortnight or so, before starting the effing training all over again.

[5]

17 November. Bromsden Farm.   On Wednesday morning I applied to be discharged from the hospital, the doctor agreed, and at 2 p.m. on Thursday (the simplest transaction takes twenty-four hours in the Army) I shook the dust of the building off my feet. I managed to get a lift back to the Depot with two nurses who were going to have their teeth examined. I found all the lads very gay and excited, as it was their last evening before moving on to Sandhurst.[1]

It took me from 8 a.m. till 1.15 on Friday to get through all the formalities and obtain the necessary bumf (leave-pass and ration-card). Then I had to be strapped into a terrific amount of equipment. First over-coat, very long and heavy. Then webbing belt with bayonet and two (empty) ammunition-pouches attached. Small haversack (stuffed with dirty clothes) on back, with neatly-rolled gas-cape on top. Gas-mask slung over right shoulder, tin hat hung over top of bayonet, *rifle* slung over left shoulder. I could scarcely move or breathe with all this on (thank God it wasn't summer), but I picked up a huge brown-paper parcel (containing more clothes etc) and trudged manfully off.

There was a red warning just before I got to the gate, but the sergeant of the guard slipped me out. After I had walked about half a mile I found a charming butcher who gave me a lift in his van (I got stuck getting in) as far as Upper Caterham. From there I walked on to the hospital, where I picked up my suitcase and slipped a bottle of beer to a chap who'd been there for ten weeks without a single drink.

As you can imagine, I could hardly carry the suitcase as well as the parcel, and my rifle kept slipping off my shoulder. Luckily a lorry-driver took pity on me and drove me to the bottom of Caterham Hill, which is long and almost perpendicular. I found all the way home that everyone is most helpful to heavy-laden private soldiers, offering cigarettes, cups of tea, and glasses of beer.

After waiting ten minutes in Caterham I got a Green Line bus which

[1] All but one of them survived the war, and one, Simon Phipps, was awarded a Military Cross and became a bishop.

deposited me an hour later at Ebury Bridge. From there I walked over to the Victoria Coach Station, and after queueing up for a time was told I couldn't get a seat in a Henley bus till next day. So I took a taxi and drove to the office. It was now about 3.30. The glass is all blown out of my room and the others in the front of the house, but otherwise all is well.

I had a cup of tea with dear old Guy, and also a short talk with Bob and Jonathan, who, as you can imagine, is now a Grade A bomb-bore. Then Guy took me to Paddington and after waiting about and having a cup of coffee I caught the 5.15 train, reaching Henley at 6.45. I was pretty well worn out by this time, as the equipment is very heavy and one can't sit back properly because of the pack on one's back.

I rang up Celia from the station and she came and fetched me. Back here first, where I had a delicious hot bath and put on my old clothes (corduroys and high-necked grey jumper). I shan't have to wear uniform again till I return on the 29th. Then Celia drove me over to Merrimoles, where we had dinner. Peter was home and it was a very gay evening. Home about 10.30.

I can't begin to describe the utter joy of being back here. I hadn't been in a private house for six weeks, or been alone, and had only one evening outside barracks and hospital. The farm is more peaceful than ever, or seems so by comparison. No guns or trenches or wireless jazz, and all the dear loveliness that we both love so. Our bed seems endlessly soft, and both nights I've slept deep and peacefully.

Yesterday I walked over to Merrimoles (to test my knee, which stood up well) and brought back our dear little car [an open Morris Minor], in which I drove Charlie and Molly down to Henley to shop. The town is now so full of refugees and evacuees that one has to fight one's way into every shop. There's not a scrap of chocolate or any other kind of sweet to be had – funny, because there seemed to be plenty in Caterham village. When I was in the train coming home I thought how wonderful it would be if you and the children were here, but really I'm so pleased and happy to know that you're all safe. Nowhere here is really so – nineteen bombs fell at Greys last week. True they only killed one cow, but it's a bit near. Ever since I got back I've been actively and consciously enjoying it all – just being here.

19 November. This morning brought your letter of 23 October. It's a long time since I last got a letter (dated 11 October), so I guess some in between have gone astray. It's wonderfully cheering to hear of the children looking so rosy and gay. With any luck the war won't touch

The children in America

their lives at all – which is more than can be said of most of the children over here.

With your letter came the wonderful parcel of sweets. They're perfectly fresh and undamaged and I'm stuffing myself with them. I hear the noise of aircraft (probably German) overhead as I write. It's 6.35 p.m. They don't seem to have the same terrors here. My nerves got a bit jumpy in the hospital, but now they're quite okay again.

Yesterday morning Charlie and I drove over to Merrimoles, taking eight empty suitcases (six large and two small). There we got into their little Ford, putting the suitcases into the trailer, which we fixed on behind. We also took Celia (who has a streaming cold) as she had to rehearse in London for the B.B.C.

It was a filthy, wet, misty, cold day (bad for driving and also for German aircraft). We couldn't go more than 30 m.p.h. because of the trailer, and with a couple of diversions due to unexploded bombs we took nearly three hours to get to Stormont Road, after dropping Celia at Golders Green tube.

I had telephoned to Nellie [who with her sister Amy was looking after the house] and she welcomed us with an excellent lunch. There have been bombs all round, but no high-explosive ones in the road itself. A few panes of glass have been cracked by gunfire, and the garden is littered with shrapnel.

Charlie and I worked like beavers, and after two hours had filled all the suitcases with my most precious and valuable books, and the back of the car with the Nicholson picture (only just got in), several other pictures and small bits of furniture, all my letter-files and locked boxes, scrap-books and other miscellanea. We must have had several tons in car and trailer when we left for home at about 2.30. There was a thick fog by then, and heavy rain. The engine of the car soon got over-heated, but by applying oil and water we managed to carry on. Eventually we got back here soon after 5 – just in time, for the trailer had no back-light. I returned car and trailer to Merrimoles and brought back our own car. Then a lazy evening and I slept the clock round.

I've now unpacked all the books and shall have to find somewhere to put them. Tomorrow I'm going up to London to get some massage from my old friend Mrs Millington. I must get my knee quite right before I go back.

Charlie says he's perfectly willing to stay on here indefinitely, but I think he'd like to get back to the theatre by the end of the year. I felt quite homesick for my whole library when I saw it yesterday, but didn't feel anything about the house. *This* is home now, and I grow fonder of it every day.

24 November. Blockley. I've now been three times to Mrs Millington (Milly to her patients), the blind lady. She said the knee was in poor condition when I first went to her. It was still swollen and bruised, two of the ligaments were out of place, and there was a dried blood-clot on the joint. All these troubles are now remedied and it feels ever so much better. She really is a wonderful woman.

After my first massage I met my pa at the Turf Club (his own having been damaged) and managed to get a first-class lunch (dressed crab, grouse pie and stewed quince). Then we sat around drinking kümmel until it was time to drive to Waterloo for the 3.45 to Petersfield. Ivor Churchill's home (where my pa is living) is a snug little house in a village called Steep. The household is most peculiar – rather like the cast of a French farce. Apart from Ivor there are two married couples (i.e. two butlers and two cooks, one couple French, one English), my pa, the painter Paul Maze and his mistress – a good-looking Scotch girl called Jessie. She has been Paul Maze's housemaid and before that Ivor Churchill's. This, as you can imagine, causes a certain amount of snobbish disgruntlement among the butlers and cooks. I must say Jessie carries the situation off with great natural dignity, and Ivor and my pa like her very much.

Ivor has a wonderful collection of French pictures, and the walls are crowded with Cézannes, Renoirs etc. Luckily Paul Maze was away the night I was there. He apparently shouts about the house, bullies the servants and bores everyone stiff. Jessie was there with a heavy cold. After dinner my pa played the piano and all went early to bed. Very comfortable and no aircraft noises. In the morning I went up to London with Ivor.

Yesterday I drove here, stopping to have a drink with E. Blunden in Oxford. All well here. Blockley is fuller than ever of refugees, and they're still pouring in from Birmingham and Coventry. Your long-lost airmail letter arrived safely at last, having taken sixteen days. If that's the usual time for airmail it's certainly a lot quicker. This is a splendid letter and I've already read it three or four times. You do write such very good letters, with just the things one wants to know.

Tomorrow we shall have been married for seven years. They say one changes completely in that time, but I love you more deeply and tenderly than ever.

Midnight 28–29 November. For days now I've been prevented from writing by one thing and another, and this is my last quiet moment before I go back to Caterham tomorrow. I had a peaceful day and night in Bath. Walter looked the picture of health, but Madge is in a very low state. They were full of reports of recent raids on Bristol, clearly visible from the top of their house. After lunch I drove Madge down into the town for a little shopping. It was seething with people and I had the greatest difficulty in garaging the car, as M & W's garage is let for the duration.

When I got back home I found two or three dreary letters and two in your hand-writing. I left them to the last, only to find that one was Bridget's darling little letter and the other those splendid photographs. On Monday I went to London for my last treatment with Milly. It's really miraculous what she's done for my knee. She says she still doesn't think it will stand much rough treatment, and she has written a statement of the facts, which I'm going to show to the M.O. in an endeavour to get out of P.T., which is where I'm most likely to damage myself.

After that I lunched with William in a pub. He was as sweet and amusing as ever. After lunch I walked back to the Admiralty with him, and on the way we saw the Queen going into the National Gallery. She was looking very charming in powder-blue, and William said: 'She gets more like her photographs every day', which I thought rather droll.

I tidied up things here a bit and then drove down to dine with the Pipers. John Betjeman was there, and we had a very amusing and peaceful evening. Charlie has got himself a good job in a Liverpool theatre, so when he and Molly pack up in December the house will be completely abandoned. It wouldn't be so tiresome if I had a few more days to fix things up, but I have to go back to Caterham tomorrow morning. Meanwhile Ruth Atkinson comes over every week-end from her job at Reading, and will probably go on coming after Charlie and Molly have left. This would anyhow ensure fires being lit sometimes.

29 November. Celia drove me to Henley, where I had some photos taken wearing all my Christmas tree accoutrements. Goodness knows what they'll look like, but they'll probably be funny anyhow. Now I'm in a very slow train, stopping at every station. However I'm not compelled to get to Caterham till 9 p.m. In fact I shall go straight on, so as to make sure of getting there in daylight.

[6]

1 December. *Caterham*. Here I am back again, and things have started with a real stroke of luck. I've been transferred to another Company, and my new Company Commander (as nice and sensible a chap as the other was tiresome and silly) at once said that, as I had already done the first four weeks of the training, he thought it quite unnecessary for me to do them all again. Accordingly he is going to give me another seven, or possibly ten, days' leave, starting about next Wednesday or Thursday. You can imagine my delight. I shall now have some chance of arranging about the farm without delaying my training here.

Secondly, I saw the M.O. (a different one) as soon as I arrived. He seemed to know much more about knees than any of the other army doctors I've seen, and put on a lot of elastoplast strapping, which he thinks I ought to wear for some time. With this and the bandage on top I find that so far I can manage the ordinary drill-movements without any pain, weakness or ill effects. The M.O. agreed that I had better be excused P.T. Both he and the Company Commander seem genuinely anxious to get me safely through my training. This enlightened attitude was as pleasant as it was unexpected.

Thirdly, my new quarters are infinitely more comfortable than the old ones. I'm in a huge solid barrack-room block on the ground floor. We have iron beds (instead of those bloody planks) with a kind of spring bottom, and a mattress (in three sections, known as 'biscuits') instead of a straw palliasse. It's hard enough, but sybaritic compared with the other. Also the lavatory and wash-house are inside the same building, we each have a decent large box to keep our own things in, there are some chairs and a table in the room (none in the old hut) and two open fires instead of a stove. Lastly there is almost no mud anywhere, our air-raid shelter is covered over and much nearer. Everything is close at hand and far more convenient, so I'm feeling very cheered and relieved.

The first night I got back there was a lot of noise overhead, and in the strange bed I didn't sleep very much. Last night, however, was foggy and silent, and I slept like a top. I find there is one ordinary pub within bounds, a very cosy one, and last night I walked there with a chap I knew in hospital and had some good beer.

The chaps in my new squad are once again nineteen or twenty, except for a schoolmaster in his thirties. They seem very nice, all of them, and both they and our new Trained Soldier look on me as an experienced old soldier who can show the others what to do. In some things, such as the shine of my boots, I'm weeks ahead of them and can sit by the fire giving advice while they polish away. Our new sergeant – his name is Jelly – seems a very nice chap, but not a patch on Sergeant Bowman in instruction, humanity or humour.

I'm writing this in the recruits' writing-room, which is warm and comfortable, has no games going on except draughts, and is almost exactly opposite our block. I rang Celia as soon as I heard about this new bit of leave, and told her to prepare Charlie for my return and tell him to hold all mail. So with any luck I should find a letter or two from you waiting for me.

The floor of the new barrack-room is polished wood, so we don't, thank goodness, have to scrub – only sweep and polish. I am in charge of a party of three who clean the lavatories every morning after breakfast, and I spend most of the time holding the door against maddened guardsmen while the others do the cleaning. They now bring cocoa round every evening, and we have to gargle once a day – both sensible innovations.

8 December.   Bromsden Farm.   What should I find when I got home but *six* letters, including two of the missing ordinary mail ones (October 17 and 20) and four air mail (October 31, November 4, 9 and 12). We mustn't worry about delays, because, so far as I can see, all our letters both ways have arrived safely *in the end*. I was speechless with excitement when I found them, but deliberately put off the thrill of opening them until I'd had a delicious hot bath and some grub, and was sitting snug by the drawing-room fire. Reading so many straight through was like hearing you talking for a long time. We've just had supper, and ate one of your Xmas puddings to celebrate Charlie's last night, as he leaves tomorrow.

I never stop missing you, but by now I'm geared to carrying on calmly with my outward life, without anyone knowing that at least half of me – the better half – is three thousand miles away. It's so lovely to be back at our dear farm, and I feel very close to you tonight.

11 December. I've arranged, if I get any leave, to eat Xmas Day lunch at the Old Gables [the Spears house near Bracknell]. They asked me to stay there now, but I refused politely, as I'd much rather be here.

On Saturday Ruth Atkinson arrived in time for lunch. Later I forced Molly to come down to Henley, where we went to the cinema and saw Spencer Tracy in *North West Passage*. I hadn't been to a film since mid-September and enjoyed it thoroughly.

On Sunday I drove over to the Old Gables for lunch. Your ma gave me a three-gallon petrol-coupon when I arrived. B.P. [as Spears was called in the family, short for *beau-père*, stepfather] was there with two sturdy A.T.S. lady-drivers. We had the usual huge meal. Your ma doesn't want to take her mobile hospital unit abroad again.

Next day I went up to London, and at the Café Royal ate my way solidly through the lunch of the day, at Guy's expense. He has been offered two separate jobs in the Army, both good. I think he'll take one [which he did], but goodness knows what'll happen to the old firm when he goes.

Then I spent an hour at the office, jawing with the boys. Jonathan grows more gaga daily, and now never stops mixing disgusting cocktails in his office. I met Daniel at Paddington and brought him down here. Molly is looking after the house till Saturday when she leaves. After that Ruth Atkinson is going to come every week-end, and Mrs Miles is coming in Saturday and Monday to light fires and clear up.

12 December. Tomorrow morning I trek off again to Caterham, taking a couple of turkeys which the squad are going to present to our two sergeants, just to keep them sweet. Now I must enjoy my last night (for a while) in a comfortable bed.

15 December. Caterham. Yesterday we all had our second anti-typhoid inoculation – a very stiff one – and have been pretty well flattened out ever since. We're excused all duties for forty-eight hours and given an extra blanket each for two nights. They say we'll feel okay tomorrow.

I've decided that, whereas at home one keeps pretty clean all the time, here one simply can't, and it's hopeless trying to compromise. It seems to me far more important to keep *warm*. Accordingly at night I simply take off my jacket and trousers, change into a special pair of socks which I keep for the purpose, and put on my thick pyjamas on top of vest and pants, shirt and two sweaters. Then, with my greatcoat on top of my army blankets I snuggle down and manage to maintain a certain warmth, though I've never yet been too hot: it's very chilly these nights. In the morning I just have to remove my pyjamas, change my socks and put on my khaki trousers, which are deliciously warm, having been pressed on my mattress all night. Lots of the other chaps employ a similar technique.

The turkeys for the sergeants were a great success. They cost thirty shillings each, and all the squad are subscribing for them equally. Bob Howard is frantic about Guy's probable departure and told Geoffrey Faber (whom I met at Milly's) that he wished to God I could come back. I've arranged with the Henley Model Laundry to post them small parcels of washing each week, which they will post back as soon as clean. The Army laundry is merciless and quite irresponsible.

I'm writing this in the peaceful writing-room, but must soon go back to the barrack-room and clean boots, rifle, sling, belt, bayonet, cap, gaiters, overcoat-buttons and gas-mask container. It seems a funny way of helping to win the war, but I daresay there are others even more tedious.

22 December.   Three lovely letters from you have arrived during the week (those of November 15, 18 and 22). Last Tuesday we duly passed the Third Week inspection once more. There was an inch of solid ice on the square, and most of the lads were slipping and falling about. The sergeant very considerately suggested to the Adjutant that, as I'd done the thing before and had my knee tied up, I should fall out and stand by during the drill. This I gratefully did, rejoining the squad for the questions on regimental history and customs, which I know by heart.

Yesterday was our first day out, and very successful too. Originally they said we could go out after mid-day dinner, but at the last minute said we must scrub out the huge gym first. When we'd done about half of it they came and said we were supposed to be moving dozens of very heavy forms into another gym for a cinema show, so we eventually got out at 4 p.m. I and two other chaps went to the house of one of the junior officers (called Doughty), where we were given a hot bath and a whisky-and-soda, both v. welcome.

Then I visited the hospital and cracked a joke with the nurses. Some
of them asked me to have a drink with them on Boxing Day, our next
day out. Then I bought some tobacco and a pack of cards in Caterham
and proceeded to our old friend the Surrey Hills Hotel, where most of
us had a good dinner and I played bridge with three of the lads. Last
night I had a lovely dream about you and me. Can't remember any
details, but I woke feeling very nice and happy.

Christmas Day. I'm sitting on my bed in the barrack-room, after a
good lunch, smoking a Romeo & Juliet cigar, and thinking of you and
our children. We had an extra hour's sleep this morning, and had
breakfast (sausage and bacon) at 8.30. Church Parade at 10.45 – a dull
short service with three good hymns (Come all ye Faithful, Hark the
Herald Angels, and While Shepherds Watch). Did I ever tell you that
when I was little I thought it was *Wild* shepherds, and was once found
pretending to be one? When we got back from church there were *nine*
presents for me, including a lovely letter from you (posted on December
5). Among the rest was a box of fifty cigars from your ma, a Christmas
box of £15 from the firm – not over-generous – and a letter from Bob
begging me to come back to the firm if my knee should crock up again.
I couldn't send you a greetings-telegram from here, so I telephoned the
office (reversing the charges) and dictated one to the telephone girl.
Besides your ma's cigars someone else sent me another *fifty*. I shall keep
most of them till I get home. I wonder who sent them. [It was Comfort.]

[7]

5 January 1941.   E Ward, Surrey County Hospital, Redhill. Yes, darling,
believe it or not, I'm in hospital again, and a very much better one this
time. On Christmas Eve John Quilter, one of the nicest chaps in the
squad, was taken to hospital very ill. Later we heard that he had
pneumonia, complicated by some mysterious bug, which caused all his
joints to swell. The authorities were so concerned about this that they
got the M.O. to examine the whole squad. We all had our temperatures
taken and our throats examined – all okay.

Next evening the trouble began. I went to a cinema-show in the
gym. It was a thrilling film called *Five Came Back* and I enjoyed it
thoroughly. But before the end my teeth began to chatter and I realised
I was in trouble. I went straight back to the barrack-room, sent one of
the lads for a mug of tea and went to bed with a brace of veganin.

In the morning I felt wretched, so reported to the M.O. after breakfast. It was really very droll, because normally they make one wait for a couple of hours before anything happens. But directly they realised that one of the suspected squad had turned up, they rushed me to the head of the queue and smothered me with blankets.

The M.O. examined me and said I'd better come straight here, so I was brought along at once, lashed tightly on a stretcher in an ambulance. It was a rather frightening journey, since I could hear the sound of planes and guns. Here I was ruthlessly blanket-bathed and then examined by a charming lady doctor. She said I'd got slight pneumonia with tonsilitis. My temperature, I discovered, was 102. I was given masses (forty tablets in all) of M & B, which did the trick miraculously. My temperature came straight down after *terrific* sweating, and has now been subnormal for days. I had a touch of pleurisy, but a delicious antiphlogistine poultice on the chest dealt with that. It all sounds much worse than it was. I was never dangerously ill, nor did I have to be given oxygen. I expect they'll keep me here for another fortnight, and then I'm pretty sure to get some more sick-leave. What will happen to my military career God knows, but I really don't care a damn either way – which is a good state to be in.

As I said, this hospital is splendid. It's run by the Surrey County Council, and *not* by the Army, which explains the whole thing. This is one of the few military wards, with thirty-six beds in it. Poor John Quilter has been lying behind a screen in the corner since he came here, at death's door, but yesterday he took a huge turn for the better, and is now out of danger. The grub's A.1. We've three times had roast chicken for lunch.

13 January. It's our tiny Bridget's birthday. Six sounds so very grown-up. Your ma has twice driven over here to see me. She brought me three detective stories and three grapefruit. Months ago she started saying she thought it was a great mistake your staying in the U.S. for the duration, but I shut her up and told her not to interfere. Now she has started up again, and I think has written to you about it. We both long to be together, but whatever happens the children must stay over there till the war's over. If you came back, who is to take complete responsibility for them? Emmy and Ham sound quite hopeless. I guess Joyce would take it on, but can you trust her? With Zlatko around? If you felt quite happy about them, then perhaps, my darling, you could come.

Here's some more about the hospital. We are woken at 6 a.m. by the wireless blaring out the News in Norwegian. Thereafter it's on all day, except when a patient is dying or dead. Then screens are put round the bed, and blessed silence reigns. At the far end of the ward there's a ping-pong table, and to a feverish patient the irregularity of the strokes is curiously annoying.

A number of bombs have fallen very near, and at night it is frighteningly noisy. The Sister rushed in once, crying: 'Don't let the pneumonias get out of bed.' I called out: 'Don't worry, Sister, we're all under the bedclothes.' One bomb fell so near that the blast blew in the outside doors at the end of the ward, and a gigantic dog walked in. An orderly came, took the dog away and fixed the doors shut. There was only one very young nurse in charge of all thirty-six patients, and as she came round I could see she was terrified, so I told her I couldn't sleep and suggested she should bring her knitting, sit by my bed and talk to me, which she gratefully did.

There is a civilian bomb-casualty in a wheel-chair who steers himself round the ward, eager to tell his bomb-story. It's astonishing how many patients are asleep when he reaches their bed.

20 January. Once again it's a week since I wrote. I was to have got up for half an hour on Wednesday, but my temperature went up again to 100 and stayed so for three nights. Now it has been all right for two. I managed to talk my way out of having any more M & B. Several of the lads from Caterham have been to see me, also my ex-secretary Jo Anderson, bringing books and papers, and yesterday the faithful Daniel came all the way from Mill Hill. I've had two letters from you this week (of December 9 and 17). When I was feverish in the middle of the week I lay dozing a good deal, and almost all the time I thought of all the lovely days and times we've had together, and I felt so cheered and calmed.

26 January. No more setbacks since last week. I'm writing this dressed and sitting at a table. In half an hour I'm going to have my first bath (as opposed to blanket ditto) since I came here, four weeks ago today. I fancy I may get out tomorrow. One of your ma's lady-drivers is coming to fetch me in a car and take me to the Old Gables. I'd much rather be at our dear farm, but I guess it's sensible to wait till I feel a bit stronger. I hear a rumour that they're going to let me go straight on to Sandhurst, without any more Caterham. Hurrah!

3 February. The Old Gables. I got out of hospital on Saturday, having been there five weeks all but a day. One of your ma's lady-drivers brought me over here in a huge Ford, and I've had a most peaceful time. I'm in bed, with a fire in my bedroom, and the aptly-named Mrs

Honey cherishing me like mad; it's all I can do to stuff down all the enormous meals she brings up to me, with hot milk and bovril in between: it's rather like being on board ship. I've got three weeks' sick-leave, and the M.O. told me that, if I didn't feel quite fit at the end of it, I was to apply for more.

6 February.   It was an excellent idea coming here, and I feel infinitely better than I did when I arrived. On Tuesday your ma dropped me off at the farm, where I spent an hour, changing into my old civilian clothes, and finding a lovely letter from you. Just before I left the hospital I went over and had a look at the children's ward. Very touching some of them were: one little mite of nine months had had its mother killed by a bomb, and its father had deserted it. It was recovering from pneumonia when I saw it and was soon going to be sent to a Barnardo Home.

9 February.   Tomorrow Celia is coming over to fetch me in her car and your ma is giving me two gallons of petrol. Last night B.P. came down, very tired and covered with medal-ribbons. The usual bickering broke out as soon as he got here, but it's not so bad as it used to be. Wartime suits B.P. He's busy and important and all that, since Winston made him a Baronet and a Major-General.[1] In my bedroom I found three little books with your signature in them – Eliot's poems, *A Shropshire Lad* and a poetry anthology. I shall take them quietly to the farm tomorrow. By the way, there's just on sixty pounds in your Highgate account. I shall leave it there indefinitely if poss.

14 February.   Blockley.   When I reached the farm from Bracknell on Monday I found *three* letters from you – the missing Xmas one (December 28), the next one (January 4), and at the same time, skipping several, the one of January 27. Since then the one of January 19 has arrived. The January 4 one was where you decided to come home, and the two later ones backed up the decision. When I went to London on Tuesday I sent you a cable saying 'Come', but when I got here on Wednesday I found your cable saying you've decided to stay put for the moment. I don't understand it, but imagine there's some good reason. From the time I got those letters, until the cable came, I was quite light-headed with joy and excitement at the thought of seeing you. I'm aching for, longing for, dreaming of our meeting. The longing for you has been steadily growing since you left, and this last illness has temporarily taken away bodily and mental strength, so it has become

[1] When someone asked Winston why he had done so much for the horrible Spears, he said: 'Louis Spears has many enemies, and only one friend, but *he* is powerful.'

almost unbearable. I haven't stressed it in my letters because I knew it was bound to make you want to come, and if the children weren't ready to be left you would be intolerably torn. Now that I know you have been, and are, as wretched as myself, truth will out.

I'm going back to the farm on Monday, just till Thursday, when I go to Caterham for *one night* (thank God) before going on to Sandhurst on Friday. If you do come, choose the safest way, however much it costs. I'll willingly repay Joyce. I don't think Lisbon is any good. You can get there okay, but I'm told it's almost impossible to get any further.

Word has just come that, after sweetless weeks, there is some Cadbury's chocolate in all the village shops. I'll try to get some when I post this. They say people are rushing for it in all directions. I really love being here: they're both so sweet and cherishing. They've got a nice girl staying, and Pop's only complaint is that 'she will leave (rationed) butter on her plate, and it's all covered with crumbs.'

15 February. Rather surprisingly Pop offers no objection to your coming back. I think they're both longing to see you. I've had a delightful letter from David Garnett, suggesting that after the war I should set up for myself as a publisher, and he would come in with me. Who knows?

18 February. Bromsden Farm. Today I set off at 9.30 a.m. (Walt Butterworth had borrowed the car and returned it full of petrol) and drove to Stormont Road. It was a nasty wet foggy day, and the drive wasn't much fun, but I was glad to see old Nellie and my books again. I went very carefully through them, picked out all the ones I wanted most and packed them into the car. Nellie gave me some good lunch, and I set off again at 2.30, arriving here at 4.30.

19 February. I have five lovely letters from you to answer (all written in January), and the sweets arrived this morning, just in time to catch me before I go back to the Depot tomorrow. I shall eat a good many today and secrete the rest for my next leave. Any minute the Pipers may arrive to spend the evening.

Later. 11.15 p.m. The best news is that I have just mastered the primus for the first time and have filled my hot-water-bottle and put it in my bed. Hurrah! In another few months I'll be able to boil an egg. The Pipers brought three rashers of bacon, I had six of our eggs, and Myfanwy fried them all on the primus. After that we had one of our tins of cherries and some gingerbreads I bought in Henley. We drank rum and hot water and then sat and talked, and they've just gone.

[8]

24 February.   *Royal Military College, Camberley, Surrey* (commonly known as Sandhurst). On Thursday I went up to London by train and lunched with my pa at the St James's Club. Because I was in battledress he took an almost pathetic pride in introducing me to all the old fossils in their deep fireside chairs. Then by train to the Depot, where I checked in all my kit, signed several forms, and then to my surprise and pleasure was told I could bugger off.

It was too late to get home to Bromsden for the night, so when I got to London (at 8.15 p.m.) I rang up John and Ernestine Carter and asked whether I could take up their oft-repeated offer of a bed for the night. Yes, they said. So I took a taxi to their little house on Campden Hill. They gave me delicious grub and a very comfortable bed. Theirs is in a reinforced basement, and mine was on the third floor. I didn't mind that, but after the peace of Blockley and our dear farm I found it too noisy for any but the most fitful sleep. Four lots of sirens (two warnings and two all-clears), guns, planes and perhaps a bomb or two kept me in uneasy wakefulness.

I rose late, cleaned my boots and buttons for the last time (a servant cleans them here) and caught a mid-day train to Camberley. Everything is wonderfully civilised after the Depot. I am sharing a bedroom with a charming fellow from the Caterham squad called Gerry Henderson. He's a rugger blue of about nineteen. Going straight from home life one would probably object to sharing a room with a comparative stranger, but after twenty-three in a hut and thirty-six in a ward it seems heaven.

The beds are quite good, there is lots of hot water, and we have a radiator in the room. One can get a hot bath (just down the passage) four or five days a week. Every evening we change into a civilian suit for dinner, and we can go out every Wednesday, Saturday and Sunday from mid-day till 11.30 p.m. I've arranged to get our car over here next Saturday.

The church parade in the morning was rather fun. We were inspected by a General and then marched past him with the band playing. During the service we sang 'Jerusalem', which I greatly enjoyed. There is a huge library here, which I shall sample this afternoon.

I reported to the M.O. when I got here. He took no interest in the pneumonia story, but showed some appreciation of my knee-trouble. I had an X-ray, which showed all bones okay, and I'm now having daily massage with an infra-red lamp. Excused P.T. for the moment, thank God.

Here, as Officer Cadets, we have gone several steps up the ladder of military caste, and are called Sir on all occasions. 'Shut up, sir,' says the Sergeant Major on parade. 'Mr Fife, you look like a bloody stuffed fish, sir.' It's really very amusing. I feel wonderfully fit so far, and don't see why I shouldn't continue so.

2 March. This place still makes a favourable impression. There's so much more freedom and spare time than there was at the Depot, and the immediate surroundings are really very beautiful: I hadn't expected that.

9 March. Yesterday I went home for a few hours. I was going to bring the car back with me, but Celia prevailed upon me to let her keep it for one more week so that she can get to Shepherds Bush, where she's making a film. So I went over by train to Reading (only half-an-hour), then bus to Peppard Common, whence Ruth Atkinson fetched me in her little Ford. I went round the garden. All crocuses out, wild daffodils in bud, wallflowers beginning to come out. It was all looking lovely.

In the evening I had drinks with Celia and Walt Butterworth, after which they dropped me at Peppard and I came back by bus and train. I was quite tired when I got back at 10.30 p.m. The station is a good mile from here, and we'd had five parades in the morning before I left. Still it's nice to know I *can* get home that way.

22 March. It's just a fortnight since I wrote to you. Please forgive me. Last week-end I was hopelessly occupied, as you will hear. Then last week I got *eight* lovely letters (February 5, 8, 12, 14, 18, 21, 24 and March 3). I sent you a cable on Wednesday.[1] As we're both sure we did right to get the children away from England, there's no reason for abandoning them, except to further our own two happinesses – or one happiness. And that, my dearest love, will have to wait till this effing war is over. Don't think the change of plan was a terrible shock to me. I had that cable and then four weeks to get used to the idea, which I have now quite done. I'm afraid some of my letters written about a month ago will have been very hard for you to bear, but you've got guts enough for *five*, my dear one, and, as you say, we must know how we're both thinking and feeling.

Since I've been here I've been perfectly tranquil and accepting.

[1] It read: ALL YOUR FEBRUARY LETTERS ARRIVED TOGETHER TODAY THINK YOUR DECISION COURAGEOUS AND RIGHT STOP HUNDRED PER CENT BEHIND YOU STOP WE WILL GET THROUGH OKAY

Occasionally, when I'm tired or momentarily dispirited, I wish to God I'd never let any of you go. But I know that is a bad and selfish feeling, and it never lasts for long. My existence is perfectly tolerable, and I can endure anything if you and the children are at the end of it. I think it was a very good thing that your longing to get home came to a head and was dispersed in that way, because the violent upheaval should have cleared the air, and from your later letters it looks as though it has.

I shall have to lay down my pen in a few minutes, as I must have an early dinner at 7.15, and then sleep in the gym, fully dressed, which isn't much fun. Air-raid precautions you know. Some months before I got here, as at the Depot, one of the buildings got a direct hit and one or two Officer Cadets were killed.

Later. Had dinner – soup, meat pie and veg, fish savoury, all good and hot. With it I drank a small bottle of oatmeal stout (sixpence). I've got a room of my own now, which is nice, although it gets no sun, as the other did. I'm still getting knee-massage most days. Last Saturday I went home by train and drove our car back here. It is now garaged in a tumbledown place just outside the gates. That night I had to go on guard for twenty-four hours. Luckily I was corporal of the guard, so had no sentry-go, only posting of sentries and guarding the guard-room. One has to stay fully dressed (with overcoat) all the time, which is very tiring. I got about three hours' sleep in the twenty-four. The other day on an exercise I was a section-leader, and my section camouflaged themselves so thoroughly on top of a little hill that the others never found us at all.

23 March. My night in the gym wasn't too bad. There was a dance going on there till twelve, and I was able to watch and drink beer. Then I slept on a stretcher. Just as we were sitting down to lunch today the sirens went and we had to dress up and double off to that effing gym again. The all-clear came soon, and after lunch I had a delicious sleep on my bed till 4, when I played bridge with three of the lads till 7.15 and won nine shillings and sixpence at twopence a hundred.

30 March. Yesterday I drove over to the farm. It's exactly twenty-one miles. I stopped in Henley, telephoned to the Pipers and asked them to tea, bought some cakes, cashed a cheque and so home. Ruth A was there. At 4.30 the Pipers came with their little boy Edward and two stray young men. So we had a huge tea-party in the dining-room. The little boy was very sweet and soon discovered the toys in the nursery. He enjoyed himself tremendously and cried bitterly when he had to go home. After they'd gone we sat snugly by the fire till 7.30, when Ruth produced some scrambled eggs and leeks *au gratin*. I left at 9.30 and crawled back here in about an hour.

5 April. Occasionally we go out for the day on some tactical scheme. We've now been here over six weeks, and have only five and a half to go. Last week our Regimental Lieutenant Colonel came down and we were all officially nominated for commissions in the regiment. We were marched in one by one, and our reports to date were read aloud. Mine said: 'A real trier. Works well and is an exceptionally nice fellow'. I nearly got the giggles.

12 April. Bromsden Farm. I'm home for one night, the first since I went to Sandhurst seven weeks ago. Ruth A has gone home for Easter, so I'm all alone here, and truly I think I'd rather be, unless I can have you with me. I drove over after lunch and bought a few bits of grub in Henley on the way. It's difficult to get much in the shops these days unless you're a 'regular', but I managed to pick up a few tins of this and that, a brown loaf, a few cakes and some salad-vegetables.

I don't know what to say about *when* you should come back, if you do. If all goes according to plan I should get two weeks' leave when I finish at Sandhurst on May 16, and then go to a camp [Pirbright], only eight miles further from here. There I should stay three or four months, but maybe not so long.

[Here I must interpolate a word about Deirdre's husband Ronnie Balfour. In 1918 he had been just old enough to enlist in the Navy; now he was back in the service and by April 1941 was a Lieutenant-Commander, working in the Map Room at the Admiralty.

On the morning of April 16 after a long night on duty in the Blitz he went to the Mayfair flat where he was lodging, only to find that it had been badly damaged during the night. Desperate for a peaceful day's rest he rang up his and Deirdre's friend Rosie Kerr and asked her if she would like a quiet day in the country. She had been nursing all night, accepted gratefully, and they set out for West Chiltington with Ronnie driving. They were both exhausted and Ronnie said 'Nudge me if you think I'm falling asleep', but tragically they both did just that, and the car crashed into a road-island on the Kingston Bypass. Ronnie was killed instantly, and Rosie was extracted from the wreckage with every bone in her face broken and other injuries, from which she miraculously recovered.

Ronnie's death and Deirdre's absence in America compelled me to look after their interests as best I could. The Army said they were going to requisition the house at West Chiltington. Knowing that everything in a requisitioned house was always either stolen or ruined, I decided that the contents of the house must be removed. To avoid the high cost of storage I had them all taken to Stormont Road, where the garage was packed solid from floor to ceiling, and the rooms in the house were so crowded that one had to edge round the furniture. In the end the Army decided not to requisition the house, and I fear Deirdre blamed me for taking all the furniture away. Later the back of their house in Wellington Square was damaged by a bomb, and I had to arrange for repairs – no easy job in those days of destruction, and difficult to combine with my military duties.]

20 April. Bromsden Farm.   Don't worry about my having to kill some Germans. Officers don't carry any weapons except a revolver, with which it's almost impossible to hit anything. You ask what we do besides parades – lectures on all sorts of military subjects, tactical schemes out of doors, trench-digging, bridge-building, river-crossing, map-reading, truck-driving, motor-bike ditto, shooting with various weapons, wire-entanglementing, road-blocking etc. Happily I'm still excused P.T.

On Wednesday I drove to London and ordered about £90 worth of uniform. Very smart it's going to be. Then I drove to Stormont, filled up the car with my best folios and quartos and took them to the Pipers, who are very kindly going to house them for me.

26 April. Sandhurst.   On Tuesday I got the day off for Ronnie's funeral. To London early by Green Line bus. Breakfast at Lyons Corner House, then joined my pa at his club. Discovered that at the last moment the funeral had been changed from London to West Chiltington (as Deirdre had wanted), and it was now too late for us to get there in time. Instead we went to the requiem mass at Farm Street. It was all rather depressing – a number of dim Balfour relations, a chubby old priest mumbling the mass, my pa and I in the front row, never knowing when to sit, stand or kneel. Later I nipped into 90 Piccadilly and saw dear old Hugh. He seemed a bit shaken by the Blitz but quite cheerful. Harold was with him.

I tried on my uniforms, filled the car with books and decanted them *chez* Piper. Less than three weeks now before we pass out. We're getting up a concert for our last night and I'm supposed to be writing a good deal of it. Hard to follow William Douglas-Home, who produced a splendid show for the last company.

1 May.   On Monday morning we had to stand about for hours, in a biting wind, and I gradually began to feel feverish and shivery. At lunchtime I went to bed and stayed there, sweating and sleeping till about 9 p.m., when I took my temperature and found it to be over 101. I sent one of the lads down for my friend the M.O., who was very kind and took me to the tiny hospital in the grounds, where I've been most days for massage. They made me thoroughly comfortable, and after sweating and sleeping all night I woke with my temperature normal, which it has been ever since. A mysterious kind of one-day flu. Got up yesterday and am going back to work today. I've enjoyed the two days' rest.

There's a rumour that the King and Queen are coming down this evening, and the whole place is buzzing with excitement. The Queen may come to the little hospital, so the two of us who are being discharged today are being kept in till after tea, so as to make the hospital look as busy as possible. One chap who has piles was told to tell the Queen he'd sprained his ankle, if she asked what was the matter with him. All the lads are going to be working like blazes when the Monarchs arrive. *Later.* The royal pair inspected the whole damn place *except* the hospital. All that fuss and subterfuge for nothing.

4 May. Bromsden Farm. My week-end party has been a great success. William couldn't come, so it consists of Ruth A, Daniel, Cecil Day Lewis and Jo Anderson my former secretary. They arrived yesterday, and after supper we all went down to the Pipers, where Cecil sang Tom Moore songs very agreeably. Today we all slept late. Cecil said, 'All wallflowers smell like flit [an insecticide]'. I told him you could trust a poet to remove the charm from all objects of beauty. He and Daniel are in excellent form, and I hugely enjoyed seeing them both – such a nice change from the military gents. The pheasant is still sitting on her twelve eggs behind the poppy in the herbaceous border.

I nearly forgot an important bit of news. Celia has produced a charming friend called Diana Gamble, who wants somewhere to live. Her husband is a prisoner in Germany and she has a little boy of fourteen months. She came over this morning and seemed to like the house. She would look after house and garden and keep a room for me. I shall be delighted if she decides to come. It's to be fixed up next week-end.

11 May. Sandhurst. This is probably the last letter I shall write you from here. Our passing-out parade is next Friday, and we drive away, dressed as officers, on Saturday morning. Diana Gamble, nurse and child, are definitely going to live at the farm, starting next week. This

Officer's Uniforms

Morning

Evening

is a smashing stroke of luck, as they will look after house, garden and chickens. I'm going to try and move a bit more stuff down from Highgate.

16 May. Cable. OLD BOY NOW AN OFFICER VERY SMART AND WELL BLESSINGS HART-DAVIS

[9]

22 May. Blockley.   The last couple of days at Sandhurst were a riot of general jollification. On Thursday evening our concert took place. I had written most of it, produced it all, and acted as compère as well. It was a thundering success and lasted for just on two hours. Mostly topical skits, dirty jokes, jolly tunes, and imitations of the officers. Friday was our passing-out parade, a fine ceremonial drill, ending with the Adjutant riding his horse up the steps in front of and into the main building. I made my pa come over and he thoroughly enjoyed it.

Next day I drove to Pirbright to sign on, then over to Steep for twenty-four hours, then Bath, stopping on the way for tea with old G. M. Young near Marlborough. On Monday I drove back to the farm, where Diana Gamble and some friends have already dug most of the vegetable garden and spring-cleaned the house. Tomorrow I've got a van bringing down from Stormont all our nice china, glass and cutlery, six chairs, the red-topped desk, one armchair, most of the linen, the chest, the tea-table and some odds and ends. All for five guineas! I'll be very relieved when it has arrived safely.

25 May. Bromsden.   Since I wrote from Blockley I've driven back here, drinking a glass of beer in Oxford with Edmund on the way, and got back just in time to receive the furniture van from Highgate. Another lovely letter from you yesterday – eleven days (May 13–24). I always wish I could stay here longer, but I gather one can get pretty frequent week-ends from Pirbright, though they say the petrol ration's going to be drastically cut.

I've visited our Bank Manager and arranged to borrow £100 from the bank, against the security of my insurance policies, to help me tide over the payment for my uniforms (£100, and the grant is only £35).

When I went to London to arrange about the furniture I took Celia out on a spree. Lunch at the Ivy (hors d'oeuvres, liver & bacon, trifle, cigar). The restaurant was packed – the first smart one I'd been to since God knows when. I flashed my uniform about a good deal. Then we went to a most amusing film called *The Lady Eve* with Barbara Stanwyck and Henry Fonda.

[My next letter, describing my arrival at Pirbright has not survived. To begin with I shared a room with Julian Paget and we had a first-rate servant, Guardsman Thatcher. In civilian life he had been a chauffeur-valet, with a bit of gardening thrown in. I managed to hang on to him, and he stayed with me until my demobilisation in October

1945. When we arrived there was only one notice on the board outside our room, which read: 'In future on receiving the order Remove Head-dress all ranks will cry Hip Hip Hurrah and not, repeat *not*, Hip Hip Hurray'.

I very soon met the man who became my greatest army friend and benefactor. Cuthbert Fitzherbert had fought with the Regiment in the Great War, and then became a big-shot in Barclays Bank. Now he was a Captain, commanding a Company, and in charge of all the training in our part of the camp, which we shared with the Scots Guards, though we never saw them except in the Mess.

Cuthbert Fitzherbert

Cuthbert had permanent spies at Sandhurst, who advised him which cadets to ask for. I had been so picked out and soon became his assistant and second-in-command. One of his most amusing inventions was a Demonstration Platoon which showed new arrivals the way to do certain things, and the way *not* to do them. Very soon after I got there he was sent away on a course and I had to run the Company and the training – a nerve-racking but valuable experience.

Early on we were given a talk by a charming Major about regimental customs. Never refer to the Commanding Officer as the Colonel or the C.O., never say Coldstream*s*; never call our servants batmen; hats can be worn at breakfast; if wearing a brigade tie in civilian clothes the dark blue stripe must be at the top of the knot; never refer to London as Town, and so on. Just as we were leaving he called us back, saying: 'There's something important I forgot to tell you. Never wear pink out hunting when the Court's in mourning.' The irrelevance of this remark, at a time when the Germans were over-running Crete, affairs in the Mediterranean looked desperate, and the lads' chances of fox-hunting remote, was both funny and splendid, showing that regimental customs held firm in any emergency.]

8 June. Bromsden Farm.   My plan of writing to you every Wednesday, as well as at week-ends, was defeated this week by dear old Hugh's death. As you probably know, he died suddenly last Sunday morning. He'd been ill for only five days, but on Saturday he fell into a diabetic coma. They got him out of that, but then his heart gave out suddenly. He had only a moment or two of pain, and he certainly didn't know he was dying, which I'm glad about. I didn't hear the news till Monday morning, when I immediately asked the Commanding Officer for three days' leave to attend the funeral and start looking after all the business. This he very kindly granted.

That afternoon I drove up to Richmond and dined with Alan and Josephine Bott (Alan and I are the executors and trustees). Then Alan and I caught the night-train to Keswick. I had managed to get a free railway-ticket (first class) from the Army. There were no sleepers, but we managed to get a carriage to ourselves, and each lay down on one side. I didn't get a great deal of sleep, and we had to change at Penrith very early in the morning.

Harold met us at Keswick. He looked terribly tired, but was outwardly calm as ever. Brackenburn was looking too lovely for words, the garden ablaze with flowers. Hugh's brother and sister were there, also the two servants, Jack and Edith, who looked after us on our holiday. They asked a lot about you and the children.

We spent all Tuesday, and Wednesday morning, sorting through letters, papers and documents – very exhausting and sorrowful. Hugh left me £100 and a picture of a girl by Marie Laurençin. Harold is left £10,000 and the two motor-cars. Except for a number of bequests to the Tate Gallery and a few individuals, we are directed to sell everything and give the proceeds equally to the brother and sister. We've persuaded them to keep on Brackenburn, with the servants and all the books and pictures in it, until the end of the war, as it would be idiotic to try and sell anything now.

Hugh left two completed novels waiting to be published, and two-thirds of another. As you can imagine, there's a terrific lot of work to be done over the whole business. I felt terribly sad all the time, both because of Hugh and remembering that lovely happy holiday we had up there.

The funeral was on Wednesday afternoon at St John's Church, Keswick. The sun was shining and everything was as it should have been. A simple service and masses of flowers. I put a bunch of tulips from the Brackenburn garden on the grave from you and me. I was sure the old boy would like that best.

We travelled down on the night-train. No sleepers again, but luckily the train stopped somewhere for three hours because of an air-raid, and we got to Euston at 7.30 instead of 4.30, a filthy hour. I slept soundly. Then we went to Hugh's flat, where I shaved and had a bath, and we looked through everything there. Then I visited Hugh's publishers, Macmillan, lunched with William (tired but in good form) and returned to Pirbright.

Diana Gamble is now in full occupation here, and very well she's doing it. She looks after me marvellously at week-ends – good grub, breakfast in bed and goodness knows what. It pleases me very much to see the place being looked after and kept clean.

Diana Gamble with her son Robin

11 June. Pirbright. Peter is home. He was wounded three times getting away from Greece – in the head, leg and shoulder – but they were all just deep cuts from splinters and have completely healed. I've got him to come down here the day after tomorrow, to give a talk about his experiences to the boys. And I'll see him again next week-end.

This afternoon they made us go through a strong concentration of poison-gas without our respirators. Bloody nonsense I call it. It was a nose-and-throat gas which makes one feel like hell for about an hour – fearful irritation in nose, eyes, throat, lungs etc, headache, toothache and feeling sick – very jolly. I've quite recovered now, after two large doses of rye whisky, which to my delight I found in the Mess.

15 June. Bromsden Farm. I've mown all the grass today, weeded the lavender, netted all the fruit and weeded elsewhere. I love working in the garden – it seems to be the one constructive thing I can do these days which has anything to do with us.

22 June. Here I am in the middle of a heat-wave. On Thursday (a sub-tropical day) we had a *twenty-mile* route-march, wearing tin hats, full fighting equipment and carrying rifles. I managed to stick it for something over thirteen miles, and then my bandaged knee grew so painful that I got leave to fall out and flagged a lift back in a truck. Next day my knee was pretty well okay, but it enabled me to escape an all-night exercise. Apart from marching, any sort of uniform is terribly hot these days, and it's a blessed relief to get over here and into my old clothes for a bit. Everyone is very excited today about the German attack on Russia, and we're all waiting to hear what Winston says tonight.[1]

2 July. Pirbright. The heat is still pretty fierce, and the grub here delicious. Last night's dinner was clear soup, fillets of sole, boiled chicken and rice, strawberries & cream and cheese. So you needn't worry about my being half-starved. Maddeningly the other day I lost my spectacles. The shop where I got them was long ago blown to bits, but luckily I had the prescription, so had another pair made (for two pounds ten shillings) in Camberley. While they were being made I had to rely on the free pairs I got from the Army. They cut the nose and distort the vision, but they do at a pinch (which is exactly the word). Tomorrow I've got leave to spend the day in London, so as to do some business concerning Hugh's estate, sign all sorts of things at the lawyer's etc.

---

[1] For his stirring speech, see his book *The Unrelenting Struggle* (1942), p. 176.

6 July. *Bromsden Farm.* I had a busy day in London – went to the office, saw everyone there and did a good deal of telephoning. Then I tried to get you a regimental brooch for your birthday, but discovered that you're not allowed to send any jewellery out of the country. It was then about noon and sweltering hot, so I walked to the Garrick Club and had a long cold delicious gin drink. There I met Michael Arlen, who was very amusing, and Charley Evans, more shaky than ever. At 1.15 I met dear old Jamie at the Ivy. He is now in civilian clothes again, but is still called Captain. He was very sweet, but in one of his rather *distrait* moods. The Ivy was packed and, it seemed, with exactly the same people as of old. At the next table to us were Clemence Dane (gigantic in black) and Dick Addinsell. Also present were Noel Coward, Fay Compton, James Agate, Peter Quennell, Cyril Connolly and so on. Also Dick de la Mare and the whole male staff of Faber & Faber, including T. S. Eliot.

Then I went back with Jamie to the Ministry of Information, where I managed to see Cecil, John Carter, and Kenneth Clark, whom I consulted about the disposal of Hugh's pictures. Then I went round to Hugh's solicitors, where we had an executors' meeting, myself, Alan and the lawyer. Then a couple of drinks with Alan at the Carlton, and joined John and Ernestine Carter at the Piccadilly Theatre, where we saw the second night of the new Coward play *Blithe Spirit*. It was very droll and I laughed like mad, though it isn't really a very good play. It lasted from 6.30 till 9.15, and after it the Carters gave me some more grub at the Ivy. Then I dashed in a taxi and caught the last train back to camp. I was a bit tired by then, but I enjoyed the day very much, and it made a nice change. It's still terrifically hot and sunny today. Why do we have the wonderful summers only in wartime?

9 July. *Pirbright.* Even to see a letter from you in my pigeon-hole here sends my heart bounding, because it's a tiny part of you, and also I think because, subconsciously, I have a sneaking desperate hope that you may be announcing your homecoming. And yet, you know, rationally it's idiotic even to propose your coming, through all the difficulty and danger. So head and heart battle on, inconclusively, and only one thing stands firm and sure – our love for each other.

[10]

On this loving note our year-long exchange of letters ended. There must have been two or three more, but only one of them has survived.

Comfort's part in our separation was much more difficult than mine. I was a tiny cog in a huge machine, doing what I was told, going where I was sent, but she had to make all her agonising decisions alone. Her letters are as detailed as mine concerning our daily lives, but hers are full of courage, self-knowledge, honesty and love. From the moment she landed in America she never ceased longing to come home, and finally her heart overcame her head. She left the children with Joyce, and on 22 July wrote to me from a Baltimore hotel:

> Beloved, I am sleeping here tonight, and tomorrow early I get on a plane to come home to you. If I don't get to you, you must know absolutely that I did not try to come just for your sake – it is for mine too. I can no longer abide with you so far away. And I am not a bit afraid – just calm and happy, darling. If I should be killed you must see to our children for both of us, unless you are killed too. You must not brood and let yourself be no good to them. I love you and them. That's all, darling.

This brave and moving letter didn't arrive for several weeks, and I particularly enjoyed 'unless you are killed too'.

Next morning she embarked on a Sunderland flying-boat at Baltimore. The authorities feared that the plane might be too heavy-laden to take off, and they had prepared a list of those who were to be disembarked if this happened. First on the list was the Ambassador's wife's lady's-maid, and Comfort was second. As the huge machine rushed across the waters of Chesapeake Bay, she repeatedly said, half-aloud, 'Get up, get up, *get up*', which at last it obligingly did.

The first I heard of all this was in a note from the Orderly Room saying: 'Mr Hart-Davis, your wife has landed near Bristol and will be at Reading Station at noon.' I immediately got leave and arrived at Reading in time. When she got out of the train we simply clung to each other in silence, with tears racing down our cheeks.

I drove her to Bromsden, where she had so longed to be. I wondered how she and Diana would get on, but I needn't have worried, for they took to each other at once, and lived there peacefully together for the next four years. After our year of enforced celibacy we made love passionately and often whenever I could get home.

[11]

Shortly after this the regimental authorities decided that, although the Regiment already had five battalions in the field, they needed a sixth. It took some time to allocate all the officers, warrant officers, N.C.O.s and men, but when the list finally appeared the Commanding Officer was W. S. (Bunty) Stewart Brown, Captain and Adjutant *myself*, who had been commissioned only a few months before. I knew nothing of Orderly Room work, but was told I should soon learn.

The logistical problem of moving eight hundred men from five or six places to five or six other places in and around Harrow-on-the-Hill in one day was considerable. To work out this complicated business I was given an office in the Holding Battalion in Regents Park Barracks and great assistance from the staff there. Thatcher and I were comfortably lodged and the food in the Officers' Mess was almost as good as at Pirbright. I asked Thatcher what the food was like in the other ranks Mess, and he said: 'Very good, sir. For the first time since I joined the Army I got up from the table blowing'.

I made a reconnaissance at and round Harrow, procured a large-scale map of the area, and after weeks of work the whole operation was carried out almost faultlessly. On 24 October 1941 the Sixth Battalion, Coldstream Guards, came officially into existence, and I became a Captain, which I remained for the rest of the war.

The battalion headquarters and Orderly Room were in an evacuated boys' house called West Acre. I and one of the company commanders had comfortable bedrooms on the first floor. Our servants and the Orderly Room staff slept upstairs. When I had to turn one of the boys' rooms on the ground floor into a cell for possible prisoners, it required the minimum of alteration. The Officers' Mess was in a former boarding house across the road. Cuthbert's Company was on what Dr Johnson would have called 'a considerable protuberance', overlooking Northolt airfield, which we were supposed to be guarding.

My worries about Orderly Room procedure were soon put to rest by Orderly Room Quartermaster Sergeant Freddy Mole. His knowledge and experience were matched by his kindness, and from him I learnt everything that was going to come in so useful in the coming years.

One day, among the pile of papers on my desk, my eye caught the words Vokes-Dudgeon. Assuming that it was some kind of gun I passed it by. Soon afterwards a very timid-looking padre turned up. His name was Peter Vokes-Dudgeon, and at the training college for padres he had been told: 'God help you if you're attached to the Brigade of Guards'. No wonder he looked timid, but in no time he became popular with all ranks and was happy in his work.

Luckily our Commanding Officer, Colonel Bunty, a charming, gentle and sympathetic man, was an Old Harrovian, which gave us a flying start in the school. All the masters and officials were friendly and helpful. It was a blessing living in Harrow, since it is on the London Underground and thus made visits to Hugh's lawyers etc much quicker and easier. On the other hand the journey to Bromsden Farm took a great deal longer.

Bunty Stewart Brown

Meanwhile Comfort settled happily, busy in house and garden. The first thing Diana remembers her doing was scrubbing the kitchen floor. She soon got a part-time job helping with milking on the farm, for which she received an additional eight ounces of cheese a week as an agricultural worker. But my Orderly Room duties and the distance from home kept us sadly apart.

I made great friends with Michael Kenyon, who was in charge of the battalion transport. He used to drive me round the Companies in a tiny car, in which we only just fitted. By the troops we were known as Rupert and the Bear. He had a fine sense of humour and a thorough knowledge of machinery. I attended a lecture he gave to his staff, in which he described, slowly and with the utmost lucidity, the working of the internal combustion engine. I understood every word, but within a few days I had forgotten it all. Exactly the same thing had happened long ago, when Peg's brother Teddy explained to me Einstein's Theory of Relativity. The mind doesn't retain such details unless one is fundamentally interested in the subject.

During our nine months in Harrow we carried out drill-parades on the school ground, and various exercises in the neighbouring country-side. One such, to test the mobility of the battalion with all its vehicles, ran into trouble. I went on ahead with my faithful runner Guardsman Haigh, who stayed close to me on all exercises, carrying my map-case, binoculars and other oddments. In Chalfont St Peter I stood on an eminence to watch the battalion's progress through the town. To my horror the leading vehicle turned into a cul-de-sac. I dashed down, shouting to everyone to halt. As I passed one of the leading trucks I heard one guardsman say to another: 'I'll tell you what this is, mate. It's the biggest fuck-up since Mons.' Sweating and cursing I managed to get the leading vehicles back in front of the main stream. The citizens of Chalfont St Peter mingled their irritation with amusement.

Early in June 1942 the battalion spent three weeks under canvas on a green hillside above Woolacombe on the North Devon coast. The Mess was in a large tent, the Orderly Room in a smaller one. I had a tent to myself with Thatcher close by. Training included advancing along the sandy beach with live ammunition fired over our heads. This seemed to me a fairly pointless exercise, since, although we learnt the sound of flying bullets, all the fear that would accompany them in battle was absent, since we knew there was no chance of our being hit.

Training started early in the morning, and a daily siesta for all ranks was ordered every day after lunch. The weather was lovely and, instead of lying down, I used to take a book, clamber down to the beach, have a refreshing bathe and then lie on the sand, reading or dozing.

On the way home at the end of the third week I escaped death by inches. Having seen the main body off in trucks and buses, I left the rear-party to clear everything up, and set off in a vehicle known as a P.U., which had two seats in front and a space behind. Guardsman Stenning drove, with me beside him, and Thatcher crouched behind with all our luggage and rations.

As we started to descend the steep hill (gradient 1 in 4) on the sea-road from Lynmouth to Porlock, with a cliff-precipice on our left and a green bank on our right, and I was thinking of the 'person from

Porlock' who cut off Kubla Khan in his prime, I suddenly realised we were going too fast. 'Put on the brakes,' I ordered. 'They're already on, sir,' said Stenning helplessly.

Ahead of us was a very high and steep embankment, which would have been the end of us. At the bottom of the hill, to which we were rushing at ever-increasing speed, was an almost-right-angle turn to the left, at the apex of which a huge army lorry was disembarking a lot of little men, who turned out to be Sappers. As soon as they saw us hurtling at them they scattered to safety.

I realised that our only hope of survival was to make the turn to the left despite the lorry, so at the critical moment I seized the steering-wheel from Stenning and gave it a severe wrench to the left. We got round the corner on two wheels, missing the lorry by a foot, turned two somersaults and ended upright, facing backwards, with every piece of glass in the car shattered. Stenning and I had been protected by the metal roof over us, but Thatcher, who had only a canvas roof, twice had all the luggage and rations on top of him.

Luckily he was only bruised and shocked, as we all three were. We sat down on some grass, and the Sappers emerged from cover, manhandled the wreck of the car off the road and swept up the broken glass. I asked Stenning why he had aimed at that huge embankment.

'I thought it would break our fall, sir'.

'More likely to break our necks'.

Then I took some of our tea-ration up to a nearby house and asked the charming lady who opened the door if she would be kind enough to make us a pot of tea, as three of us had had a nasty accident. 'Certainly', she said, and before long she came down with a tray on which were three cups and saucers, a pot of tea and a jug of milk. We all enjoyed the drink, and then I told Stenning to take the tray back and thank the good lady for her kindness. He took it, advanced a few steps and then dropped the whole thing on the road, smashing every-thing on the tray.

'First of all you nearly kill us, and now you can't even carry a tray a few yards.'

'It's not my lucky day, sir.'

'I should damn well think it isn't.'

I gathered up the fragments and carried them on the tray up to the house. There I explained that one of the men had been more severely shocked than I had realised, apologised humbly and said she must let me pay for replacements.

'Oh no,' she said: 'This is only a rented house.' I thanked her again and walked away, pondering her last remark. Then I managed to telephone to the rear-party and tell them to send another vehicle to pick us up. This they did, and the new driver took us most sedately all the way to Bromsden Farm, where the three guardsmen slept on the nursery floor.

Later I had to write a report of the accident and say whether I thought Stenning should be kept on as a driver. I hadn't the heart to suggest his leaving the job he loved, so I said that I thought with a little more experience he would be a satisfactory driver. Many years later, as I was crossing St James's Square on my way to the London Library, a man rushed towards me beaming.

'Do you remember me, sir – Guardsman Stenning?'

'My God, I'll never forget you. What are you doing now?'

'Still driving, sir.'

We chatted about our adventure on Porlock Hill and then parted with a warm handshake.

Soon after this the battalion moved to Eastcote, near Ruislip, still luckily on the London Underground. There we occupied some sixty little houses. Thatcher and I had one to ourselves. I had to send round an order that no bath was to have more than six inches of water in it, and waterproof high-water-marks were painted on every bath. In front of one of the little houses stood a rickety surface shelter, which was out of bounds to the troops until it was brought down by a heavy rainstorm. The memory of it brings back my favourite Blitz anecdote of Cockney wit.

The warning siren sounds. A crowd of men and women rush into a pitch-dark shelter. Almost immediately an officious air-raid warden puts his head into the entrance and calls out: 'Any pregnant women in there?' A man's voice from the back: 'Give us a chance. We've only been 'ere five minutes'.

In the middle of all our houses was an immense rubber-dump, covering several acres and containing everything from aeroplane tyres to hot-water bottles. The troops spent much of their spare time prodding in it for treasures.

[12]

In September the battalion made a big move across London, to a blitzed orphanage at Wanstead E.11. It was a huge, grim building and, like Caterham and Sandhurst, it had received a direct hit some time before I got there. The damage had been roughly repaired, but most of the doors and windows either didn't open or couldn't be shut. There were several lavatories, each of which contained a normal-sized seat for the nun or governess, and on each side a much smaller one for an orphan. The guardsmen were forbidden to enter these rooms.

Colonel Bunty had been transferred to the fifth battalion and was succeeded by Colonel Walter Barttelot. In all the many forms I had to fill in there was a tiny space for the Commanding Officer's name, in which I had somehow to write Lieutenant-Colonel Sir Walter de

Walter Barttelot
with his son Brian

Stopham Barttelot, Bart. Walter was a fine professional and dynamic soldier, the Army his only interest. I soon discovered that he had few friends, and as we got on very well I became almost his best friend and was godfather to his younger son. Driving about with him was a terrifying experience, since he was forever telling the driver to go faster.

He, his charming wife Pat and their infant son Brian (who later matched his father's military distinction) lived in a house just outside the orphanage grounds. There were eight hundred men in the enormous building, and only one staircase, in the middle. When there was an air-raid warning, which there was almost every night, I used to dress and go down to the guardroom at the bottom of the stairs, where I sat by the fire, drinking cocoa and talking to the men. If a bomb had fallen near us goodness knows how we could have got everybody out, but luckily it never happened.

One of Colonel Walter's first acts when he took over was to order an all-ranks cross-country run. I politely told him that this was the most unpopular order he could have given, and reported that Peter Fleming had told me about Montgomery's arrival as Commander of South-Eastern Command. One of his first orders was for an all-ranks cross-country run, with P.T. instructors stationed along the way to encourage and bully the runners. Soon the route was strewn with the bodies of elderly staff-officers and other chairbound soldiers, shamming dead or complaining of cramp, a stitch or heat-exhaustion. Stretcher-bearers were busy, and the sick-bay soon filled up. Colonel Walter was astonished by this news, but he halved the length of the run and never ordered another.

In October I had a few days' leave, which Comfort and I spent happily at John Fothergill's inn The Three Swans at Market Harborough, going for walks and to the cinema, shopping, and making love. Despite rationing Fothergill produced much delicious food.

[13]

The eventful year 1943 began with a very tiresome example of the power of chance. There was no military unit within five miles of us, and one of our duties was to send out our battalion police, backed by members of the Corps of Military Police, to search for, and if possible arrest, any deserters or absentees in a large area of north and east London. Almost every day I signed a batch of arrest-warrants without looking at the names of the absentees.

Early in February one of those arrested turned out to be Julian Maclaren Ross. In the June 1940 issue of *Horizon* I had read a short story of his called 'A Bit of a Smash', which I thought good. I wrote to him and asked him to come and see me. At our only meeting I told him that if he could write twenty stories as good as this one I was sure Cape would publish a book of them.

Now he was a lance-corporal employed in the Orderly Room of an infantry depot at Southend-on-Sea. He was arrested when he was found in bed with his girl-friend somewhere in North London. He asked to see the corporal's warrant, saw my name on it and persuaded the corporal to bring back a note to me, saying he was in close arrest and crying for help.

I drove over to Southend on Sunday and soon realised that the depot contained the dregs and chuck-outs of the army in a great many little houses. I marched into the Orderly Room, where I found the Commanding Officer, a tired old gentleman. I asked his permission to visit one of his (I imagined many) prisoners. Taken by surprise he agreed. I found Julian confined in the back room of one of the little houses, and when I was left alone with him he rushed forward in a state of great excitement, thrusting a tiny bundle into my hand and saying: 'Here are my manuscripts'. With some difficulty I forced them into my greatcoat pockets. He told me he was charged with being absent without leave for a fortnight and for stealing a box of army stationery. A summary of evidence was being prepared and he feared a Court Martial was likely. Would I defend him if this came about? Reluctantly I agreed. When I left him I returned to the Orderly Room and told the Commanding Officer that if there was a Court Martial I would come over to defend Julian. This so terrified the old gentleman that next morning he sentenced Julian to twenty-eight days' detention, the severest penalty he could inflict.

But before the sentence could begin, the psychiatrists moved in, and soon Julian was transferred to the Military (Psychiatric) Hospital at Northfields, Birmingham, which in happier days had been a lunatic asylum. Most of the officers were psychiatrists, and as they discussed his case between themselves, Julian bombarded me with letters in his tiny but astonishingly legible handwriting – five in February, seven in March, eight in April, eight in May, seven in June. At the end of March I got a day off and travelled to Birmingham to see him. He was dressed in the red, white and blue wounded soldiers' clothes, which I had worn at Redhill. It was a warm sunny day and we sat talking outside.

I wrote to the Commanding Officer at Northfields and to the one at Southend, telling them that Julian would only be an expensive liability in the army, and they would do well to discharge him. Eventually in May the psychiatrists decided that he should be discharged, but the Army insisted that he should first do his twenty-eight days' detention, and he was sent to Colchester, where he suffered until 13 May, when he was returned to Southend, but it wasn't until 5 July that a medical board graded him E, unfit for military service, and he was a free man. In 1944 Cape published his first and best book, *The Stuff to Give the Troops*, vivid short stories about life in the lowest ranks, and, as well he might, he dedicated it to me.

[14]

Before we left Wanstead an unusual incident took place. Each battalion in the regiment has two extra Warrant Officers Class Two, who rank immediately below the Regimental Sergeant Major and assist him in drill and discipline. They are called Drill Sergeants, and we had two fine ones.

Every morning in the Orderly Room I opened all correspondence addressed to the Commanding Officer and dealt with as much of it as I could. One day there came an anonymous letter, which ran:

> 'Dear Sir, I think you should know that Drill Sergeant X has a woman sleeping in his bunk and every morning he details a guardsman to fetch her breakfast.
>
>   Yours faithfully   A Wellwisher'

When I showed the letter to Colonel Walter he said 'Good gracious, what are we going to do about it?' 'Leave it to me, sir,' I said: 'I'll have a word with the Drill Sergeant.'

When Colonel Walter had left the room I sent for the Drill Sergeant, a tall, handsome and very smart man. He stood stiffly at attention until I told him to stand easy, then I said: 'I have to tell you, Drill Sergeant, that this morning the Commanding Officer received an anonymous letter which reads as follows. Neither the Commanding Officer nor I pay any attention to anonymous letters, and I am now going to burn this. [I threw it on the fire.] Neither of us will mention it to anyone, but you must agree that conduct such as is reported in this letter is quite unthinkable for a man in your position.'

'Yes, sir.'

'That's all, Drill Sergeant, and you need not say anything unless you want to.'

'I should just like to say, sir, that there's not a word of truth about the breakfast.'

He then sprang to attention, saluted me smartly and marched out of the room. I realised that he immediately saw the distinction between his private life and the irregular detailing of a guardsman. The matter was never referred to again.

[15]

Then the regimental authorities decided that there were too many battalions, and the sixth, which was by now fully trained for battle, was to be disbanded and distributed, company by company, as reinforcements for the battalions in the field. This was a blow to me, since if the battalion had gone abroad as a fighting unit I could and would have gone with it as Adjutant. But nobody wanted a platoon-commander of thirty-five, so I was out of a job. There was talk of sending me to the Staff College, but the waiting list proved to be impossibly long, so I was given a job as a Staff Captain Q at the Headquarters of London District and the Brigade of Guards at Leconfield House in Curzon Street.

This had one advantage: Thatcher and I were able to live at 32 Stormont Road, lovingly looked after by the two old sisters, Nellie and Amy. Nellie was a non-stop talker, and her anecdotes were so long that one quickly lost the thread. One evening she was rattling away, and I was not really listening, until I heard her say 'Amy was feeling poorly, so we opened a tin of crab'. Let us hope it did the trick.

Every morning I went to work by underground – Archway to Green Park, whence I walked up Curzon Street, always leaving time to look in at Heywood Hill's bookshop, which was then being run by Nancy Mitford. She was angelically kind to me, taking immense trouble to get me any new books that I wanted and advertising for old ones.

The job itself was excruciatingly dull and mostly pointless. Innumerable files, stuffed with useless and out-of-date documents, passed from hand to hand. The only bright spot was the presence in another part of the building of my friend Nico Llewelyn Davies, the youngest of J. M. Barrie's adopted sons, who brought joy and laughter wherever he went.

I usually lunched at the Guards Club, and once I took Priestley as my guest. He was apprehensive, feeling sure the officers would abuse and throw him out as a left-wing radical. We had a drink at the bar and a good lunch, without a single member paying the least attention to us, but when we were having coffee in a large sitting-room, an aged waiter tottered up to us and said: 'Excuse me, Mr Priestley, sir, but I should like to thank you for the great pleasure you have given me with Jess Oakroyd and all your other characters.' Jack was clearly delighted and thanked the old man gruffly. I apologised for the club's failure to live up to his expectations.

One of the most tedious of my duties was to accompany a high-ranking officer in the A.T.S., a stern lady with red and gold on her uniform, to the inspection of A.T.S. living-quarters, of which there were a large number in Greater London. Every lavatory had to be inspected, and in each I pulled the plug. If it flushed the lady put a tick against it in her list, and when, much more often, it failed to flush, she put a cross. Day after day of this did seem to be an obscure way of helping the war effort.

[16]

As a break from this wearisome activity I made friends with an illustrious and delightful man, Field-Marshal Lord Wavell. Peter Fleming, who was on his staff in India, joined with Lady Wavell to persuade her husband to submit to Jonathan Cape the anthology of poetry which he had compiled during his life. It was called *Other Men's Flowers*, and Jonathan sent Wavell a cold and half-hearted response, which would have made most authors withdraw the book at once, but Peter cautioned delay, sent me by airmail a copy of Jonathan's letter and an urgent request to put matters right, as Wavell was coming to London for consultation with the Government. I wrote Jonathan a frank and brutal letter,[1] and then telephoned and told him that I would look after the whole matter, since I was still a director of the firm, and luckily still had an army job in London. After Wavell's arrival I lunched with him a number of times at the Army and Navy Club (commonly called The Rag) and visited him and his wife at their apartment in the Dorchester Hotel. One day Lady Wavell took me aside and begged me to persuade her husband to include in the book a lovely little poem of

[1] See *Jonathan Cape, Publisher* by Michael S. Howard (1971) pp. 177–8.

his own. This I finally succeeded in doing, and it duly appeared as a coda to the anthology.

I was immediately impressed by Wavell, with his rugged face, his one eye (the other shot out in battle) and his immense integrity. He had no small talk, for which I was grateful, but on poetry and his book he spoke freely and with great feeling and humour. When I asked him whether he'd like to appear on the title-page as A. P. Wavell, as in his life of Allenby, or as Field-Marshal Lord Wavell, he thought for a little and then said 'Everybody *calls* me Archie'. I said: 'I think, sir, that would look a trifle frivolous on the title-page', and he eventually agreed to A. P. Wavell, with his title and decorations in brackets underneath.

I also persuaded him to write notes about as many poems as possible. He wrote them wherever he was – in London, in an aeroplane or in India, and sent them to me, with an occasional extra poem or two. During the time of our meetings he was appointed Viceroy and Governor General of India. *Other Men's Flowers* was published by Cape in March 1944, received glowing reviews, was a Book Society Choice, and sold tens of thousand copies during several decades.

INTERLUDE : A JOYFUL ERRAND

Come, dear children, let us away.

M ATTHEW A RNOLD

[1]

M EANWHILE ON 4 July 1943 our son Adam was born at Bromsden Farm, with Sister Cooper in attendance. It was exactly nine months since our holiday at Market Harborough.

Ever since Comfort came home, and even after the birth of Adam, she had been pining for Bridget and Duff. We were informed, on good authority, that it would now be safe for them to come home in a neutral ship, looked after by an Englishwoman who would be grateful to have her fare paid. I accordingly wrote to Joyce, asking her if she would be kind enough to make the necessary arrangements. She refused to do so. I felt sorry for her: she had no children of her own, loved ours, and thought that if they weren't torpedoed they would be starved in England. I wrote again, saying that they were our children, and Comfort and I wanted them at home.

She then played her last card, sending a certificate from a venal doctor saying the children were too ill to travel. This I knew was nonsense, so I decided I must go and fetch them myself. Accordingly I marched in to General Sir Arthur Smith, the General Officer Commanding London District and the Brigade of Guards (luckily he was a Coldstreamer) and asked for compassionate leave to rescue my children from America. He was astonished and said he'd never received such a request before. I outlined my problem, and I saw he was weakening when he said: 'I can't get you there, you know.' 'Yes, sir,' I said: 'I shall have to find my own way there.' Then he said: 'Oh well, I suppose you'd better go.' Blessing him silently I produced a document which I had persuaded a clerk to type on official paper, saying 'I have given Captain R. C. Hart-Davis compassionate leave to travel to America', and he signed it like a lamb. Finally I said: 'You realise, sir, that I can't tell how long I shall be away, and you'll have to trust me to return as soon as I possibly can'. 'All right, all right,' he said, shooing me out of the room.

I then encountered what in later days was called the Catch 22 situation. I couldn't get a passage on a ship until I had an exit-permit, and I couldn't get an exit-permit until I had a passage on a ship. After several days of vain endeavour I joined an enormous queue outside the War Office, and after standing there and shuffling forward for three or four hours, I was admitted at five p.m. to the presence of a Major Turner (may his name be forever blessed). He had clearly been dealing with every sort of problem all day and looked desperately tired.

'Oh God, what do *you* want?' he asked. I said 'A passage on a ship to America to rescue my children', and showed him the General's authority for compassionate leave. Without a word Major Turner took a piece of War Office paper and typed on it an order. 'You will embark on the Clyde at 0930 hours [in a few days' time]'. He signed and stamped the document and gave it to me. I thanked him profusely as the next applicant was ushered in.

An exit-permit followed naturally, and during the last week of July I embarked on the *Mauretania* in the lower reaches of the Clyde. I reported to the ship's adjutant and was told I should have to pay £25 for my passage. I gave him a cheque and asked if I was the only human being on board who was paying for his passage. He said he thought that was so. 'In that case,' said I, 'couldn't I have a cabin to myself?' He said I could.

In the ship's canteen I bought a little black notebook, in which I began a daily diary. I only wish I had written in it for longer.

26 July. So far the voyage has been uneventful and unexpectedly comfortable. As a result of having paid for my passage I have a cabin to myself with running water. Most of the others are from six to nine in a cabin. The food is plentiful and excellent. Particularly 'memorable' to the ration-conscious are the oranges, grapefruit, apples, also the large pots of butter and bowls of sugar on the table. At the canteen biscuits, sweets, chocolate and cigarettes are available *ad lib* and very cheap. The ship is dry, and the bottle of whisky I brought with me is locked in a suitcase for secret drinking.

I reckon there are about five thousand souls on board, of whom two thousand are ex-members of the German Africa Corps. Of the cabin passengers some hundreds are naval and merchant service officers, going over to fetch new ships of all kinds – destroyers, frigates, aircraft-carriers, mine-sweepers, corvettes, merchantmen and goodness knows what. There are also a few soldiers (English, U.S. and Canadian) and airmen. Also about thirty women and children.

Yesterday the sun came out and I lay all day on deck on a box of emergency lifebelts. Since the ship pursues a zigzag course, to avoid lurking submarines, one is alternately in and out of the sun. I brought with me *The Cloister and the Hearth*, now three-quarters finished, but I have been seduced by the ships' library into reading *The Squire* by Enid Bagnold (a lovely book), *Blessington-D'Orsay* by Michael Sadleir (entertaining), and H. V. Marrot's *Life of Galsworthy* – not a book at all but a hotchpotch of material, in which the Garnett letters interested me greatly. Galsworthy had no sense of humour, and only a limited amount to say. Nor was he flexible enough to notice the flux of time, so that he began as a 'Radical' and, simply because the world changed and he did not, ended up as a repetitious and played-out Conservative.

27 July. Spent most of the day in my cabin opposite the electric fan. Read another hundred pages of *The Cloister*. The end is now in sight, and I quite want to know what happens. All the same it has been pretty tough sledding. I believe this book and *Lorna Doone* are the two most generally popular English novels, and I felt I must tackle them both. Taylor of Dent's told me that *Lorna Doone* has proved easily the best selling of all the 950 titles in the Everyman Library. I embarked on it in hospital at Redhill, without much else to read, but got hopelessly bogged down about half-way through. *The Cloister* is lighter and less heavily, locally, romantically bogus.

We get scarcely any news on board. Each morning at 11.30 a bulletin is read out, but we've now put back the clocks so often that we scarcely know which day's events are in question. Yesterday we were simply told that Mussolini had fallen, but how much is involved in his fall we don't know.

I have made friends with some very nice naval officers, especially two who were at Eton. During the turbulent ten days I spent arranging for this trip I learnt once again that Eton and the Brigade of Guards are two of the most powerful trades unions – almost secret societies. Hamish Mure Mackenzie of the Fleet Air Arm is a considerable pianist and gives a popular concert in the lounge every evening. His favourite work at the moment is Dick Addinsell's *Warsaw Concerto*, which he plays with great brio.

Later. After dinner (6 p.m.) today a great white Flying Fortress circled round and round the ship, signalling with light-flashes in its nose. It seemed to be showing off rather than patrolling.

The German prisoners live on E Deck or lower, but are brought up for air, a thousand in the morning, ditto in the afternoon. There they are crowded into a tiny space, where they sit or stand, talking and smoking. They all look very blond and clean and cheerful. There are one or two leading spirits with a fiddle and an accordion, who give concerts and start community singing. They got a terrible fright when, half-way across the ocean, all the anti-aircraft guns on the deck were fired, to make sure they were in working order. The prisoners thought the ship was being bombed and might well have stampeded if they hadn't been surrounded by some ramshackle Canadians flourishing Bren guns and fixed bayonets.

28 July. Finished *The Cloister* yesterday with a certain quiet triumph. I think it *very* unlikely that I shall ever read it again. Spent all morning leaning over the forward rail on the upper deck, watching first buoys, then seagulls, then boats and so on, until we anchored off Quarantine at noon. The prisoners were removed in an army tender. We docked about 4 p.m., and through the good offices of a glib little man called Captain Dunn, the army officers got right through immediately, without any examination or formality. In the next berth lay, bottom up, the remains of the huge French liner the *Normandie*, which had been sabotaged and destroyed in February 1942.

I telephoned to Deirdre at the British Information Services, where she worked and had all day been rushing round the building, crying 'My brother, my brother'. She looked lovely and just the same as three years ago. Went with her to her apartment, which is over a fish restaurant at 121 East 52nd Street. It is small but comfortable. We were both too excited to talk coherently. We dined with friends of hers and got to bed about 1 a.m. It is very hot. And so the first part of my rescue operation is safely over.

[2]

29 July. In the morning I telephoned to Joyce, telling her I was in New York and would be coming to Maine in two days' time to fetch the children. She agreed to meet me with a car at Rockland. Soon after this the door-bell rang and there was Zlatko, as bouncy as ever. Without mentioning the children or Joyce or Comfort, he began to detail his present activities: 'I will tell you what I am doing for the war effort.

Persemple I am member of the Anglo-Yugoslav executive committee. Number two . . .' and so on with a list of futile and pointless activities. I was thankful when he finished and went away to join some other useless committee.

31 July. A hellish day. Thirteen hours in the train, sitting bolt upright with a streaming cold in the head, and the temperature well into the nineties. Joyce met me at Rockland at 10 p.m. and drove me to Hillside Farm, a white wooden farmhouse in tree-covered mountains, a few miles inland from Camden. I crept up for a peep at the children asleep. They looked huge, blonde and lovely. They had been five and four when I last saw them. Now they were eight and seven.

Joyce has embraced some esoteric religion in which reincarnation plays a big part. She has turned a small room into a sort of shrine, with prie-dieu, incense and various holy emblems. I was given a room in which was a contraption that was an uncomfortable settee in the daytime, and a much more uncomfortable bed at night, but I was so tired that I slept well.

In the morning there was a knock at the door, and the children came in.

Bridget: 'Hallo.'

Me: 'Hallo. Do you know who I am?'

Bridget: 'No.'

Me: 'You ridiculous children. I've come three thousand miles to see you, and you don't even know who I am.'

Bridget: 'It couldn't be Daddy, could it?'

Me: 'Yes, it could.'

They rushed at me, hugging, kissing and laughing. They were so thrilled that it was all I could do to stop weeping, and in a great wave I realised how deeply I had missed and longed for them during those three years. They never left me all day, mostly holding me by one fat hand each. I had brought a lot of toys from New York, which were rapturously received, energetically played with, and mostly smashed before we left. It was a magical day, and I was so happy that I couldn't think – just drifted about with them, loving everything so very much.

They several times asked whether they could go back to England to see Mummy and Adam, and when a day or two later (having made all the arrangements) I told them they could, they had a moment's frenzied pleasure and then without a word started packing all their favourite toys and books in little bags. They didn't seem to mind leaving anyone or anything much, except Mary, Emmy's eldest child.

Conversely, everyone was wretched at their departure. Emmy was very sweet and just the same. I got Comfort's clothes and other things from her. Ham I took to greatly.

We left Camden on 4 August in a 'drawing-room', the most comfortable sleeper on American trains. The children slept peacefully in a large double bed, while I lay sleepless on a rock-hard sofa. Deirdre was away for the first few days of our stay, but her Swedish maid Linda looked after us splendidly and provided excellent meals.

The temperature was still in the nineties, and every day I kept the children indoors in their underpants, occasionally venturing out myself to get them ice-cream. They were very good, but I got rather tired of their playing American war-songs on the wind-up gramophone. 'The Caissons are Rolling Along' and 'Coming in on a Wing and a Prayer' they played again and again.

In the cool of the evenings I took them to the Central Park Zoo, the Carousel, the Natural History Museum, Woolworth's five-and-ten-cent store, where Duff bought a small Union Jack, which he lashed to the outside of the apartment's front window. But their greatest delight was when I took them to the top of the Empire State Building. I hate heights, but their enthusiasm calmed my fears, and this expedition was the only one they remembered after they got home.

We met Gerry, the lady who was to look after them on the voyage, and arranged to meet her in Philadelphia. The sailing of the Portuguese ship was twice postponed, and we spent ten sweltering days in New York.

I had worn civilian clothes since I arrived in America, but thought it might be helpful if I wore uniform in Philadelphia. And so it proved, for when we reached the quayside there was the Portuguese ship, flying its national flag and with all its lights blazing. A huge heavily armed U.S. coastguard stood on each side of the gangplank, beside a notice which said: 'Nobody who is not travelling in this ship will go anywhere near it.' I approached one of the armed men and said: 'I'm not travelling in this ship, but my two little children are and I want to see them installed. Will that be okay?' He replied: 'Captain, the more questions you ask, the more trouble you get into.' So I strode up the gangplank with Gerry and the children, and all the Portuguese sailors sprang to attention and saluted me. Sadly I kissed the children goodbye and returned to New York.

[3]

How was I to get home? I rang up the military attaché at our Embassy in Washington and asked if he could get me on to a plane. He said he could send me to a bomber-base, but as I had no priority I might be stuck there for months, and I'd be much more comfortable in New York. Eventually, I forget exactly how, I secured a passage on the *Queen Elizabeth*, which had been built before the war but not fully fitted out, and was now acting as a troop-carrier. I've often wondered whether we should have won the war without her and her sister-ship the *Queen Mary*.

I was one of a party of twelve foreign (i.e. non-American) officers, of whom I remember a Portuguese General (him especially), a Swedish sea-captain, and a delightful old Englishman who had been over to teach the Americans how to train war-dogs. We had four cabins with three bunks in each, and each cabin had its own functioning bathroom.

We embarked in the afternoon, and as soon as darkness fell there was for many hours a continual tramp, tramp, tramp, as *fifteen thousand* American troops marched on to the ship. Five thousand of them had to sleep on the decks and were forbidden to light even a match. Theoretically at noon each day they changed places with another five thousand, but I never discovered how this huge operation was carried out.

There were two meals a day, breakfast from 6 a.m. till 2 p.m., supper from 3 till goodness knows when. I thought of the feeding of the five thousand in the Bible. These meals were the only occasions during the voyage when we could sit down. The decks were covered by a mass of men, sun-bathing, shooting craps, playing cards and sleeping. All one could do was to lie in one's bunk, where peace was shattered by a loud-speaker in each cabin, through which an American officer spoke almost continuously. We stuffed our loud-speaker with socks and towels, but the sound was still distracting, especially as the officer said everything twice.

It was an immense relief when, after six or seven days, we steamed into the Clyde, the only place where these huge ships could anchor in safety, and I felt pleased that these Americans' first glimpse of Britain was not some horrible place like Liverpool docks, but the gentle little green hills of the Scottish lowlands.

The tenders to and from the shore were the Dover-to-Calais ferries, and the troops were disembarked by units. The first was a medical unit – forty doctors, sixty nurses and a large number of orderlies. When the roll was called on the tender, one man was missing, and the dreaded loud-speaker kept on saying: 'Number 286134 Enlisted Man Jones, you are keeping the tender waiting. Hurry up, fella.' The wretched man was probably asleep in some far corner of the enormous vessel.

Realising that this process was going to last forever (I learned later that it went on for two-and-a-half days) I took the Portuguese General along to the ship's adjutant and told him: 'This General, sir, has an important appointment in London (quite untrue, so far as I knew) and he can't wait for this lengthy disembarkation. He would be most grateful if you could lay on a small boat to take him and the other eleven foreign officers ashore as soon as possible.' The adjutant readily agreed to do so, and we were soon safely landed. No customs or examinations, for which I was grateful because I had two trunks filled with oranges, nylons and a lot of other things that were unprocurable in England.

[4]

Meanwhile the children's voyage took a fortnight, and when they landed at Lisbon they were told that since June, when the flying-boat in which the actor Leslie Howard was travelling had been shot down into the sea on its way to England, the service had been cancelled. So Gerry and the children were taken to a luxury hotel at Estoril on the coast, where they spent another fortnight. As Richard Hughes wrote in his novel *A High Wind in Jamaica*, 'It is a fact that it takes experience before one can realise what is a catastrophe and what is not. Children have little faculty of distinguishing between disaster and the ordinary course of their lives.' And sure enough, even after they had eventually been flown home in a flying-boat, our children took the whole adventure as a matter of course and never referred to it again.

I had been away for six weeks when I got back to London in time to meet the children at Victoria on 14 September and drive them through the blacked-out city to blacked-out Paddington, where with some difficulty we found a Reading train. When we had bundled the children and all our luggage into what looked like an empty carriage, I suddenly saw a little man in the far corner, and who should he be but my beloved Edmund Blunden, reading Milton's Latin poems with a torch.

The family reunion at Bromsden Farm was a triumph of joy and relief. The children were thrilled to find Comfort again, and had to be restrained from trying to pick up the infant Adam. Eventually they became so over-excited that, after a hasty supper, they were put firmly to bed in their own home.

The Family Reunited Summer 1943

PART FOUR : THE LAST PARADES

His helmet now shall make a hive for bees.

GEORGE PEELE

[1]

SOON AFTER my return to Leconfield House I asked for an interview with the Regimental Lieutenant-Colonel, at which I told him that I hated wasting time as a Staff Captain Q, and begged him to take me back into the Regiment, in whatever capacity. He told me he was looking for an Adjutant for the Training Battalion at Pirbright, and since I had been Adjutant of the Sixth Battalion for eighteen months I was well qualified for the job. On 5 October, my appointment having been confirmed, Thatcher and I returned to Pirbright, where we had first met, and I took up the post which I was to hold for the last two years of the war.

I asked the Regimental Sergeant Major if there was any news. 'Nothing much, sir,' he said, 'except that a young officer, name of Knatchbull, was crouching in a slit-trench when a guardsman jumped on top of him. He's now recovering in bed'. I immediately visited the casualty, and this was my first meeting with the future Lord Brabourne, who after the war introduced me to two of the most interesting men of our time.

I quickly realised that the Training Battalion was very different from a service battalion. Instead of some eight hundred men, Pirbright at that time held almost three thousand, coming, training, going and coming back. The recently announced Python Scheme ruled that any man who had been abroad for three years or more could, if he wished, be posted to home duties. This brought many undesirables back to roost. One of the ways of getting rid of dud sergeants was to second them to some far-flung unit such as the Africa Field Force. Once there they were quickly promoted to Regimental Sergeant Major, and at one moment I had six of them of such spurious rank in the camp before we managed to fob them off on O.C.T.Us and other training establishments.

I interviewed each returning warrior before he went on leave. One day a very smart and alert man was marched in. When I had asked him how long he had been abroad, where he had served, where his home was etc, I said: 'I see you've got the initials P.P.A. on your shoulder. What do they stand for?'

'Popski's Private Army, sir.'

Here the Regimental Sergeant Major burst in:

'Put that man in close arrest for gross (pronounced to rhyme with Ross) impertinence to the Adjutant.'

'Wait a minute, Sergeant Major. I'm sure this man didn't mean to be impertinent.'

We had never heard of this intrepid band of Arab and British soldiers, organised and led by a Polish former sugar-merchant, now Lieutenant Colonel, called Vladimir Peniakoff, which had again and again penetrated far behind enemy lines in North Africa, sabotaging vehicles, releasing prisoners of war, and setting up an intelligence network.[1] All this the indignant man explained to us.

The R.S.M. was an alert and friendly man from Derbyshire, known as Nippy Kirk. On my first day back at Pirbright I had a long talk with him. I told him what he knew already, that I was only a temporary officer who had some experience of work in the Orderly Room, but still had a tremendous lot to learn, which I relied on him, with his long experience, to teach me. We agreed never to let each other down, and our friendship lasted firmly for two overworked years.

The Commanding Officer, H. M. (Tim) Sainthill, was a delightful man. He had been awarded a D.S.O. in North Africa, but administration was not within his compass, and to control and administer this enormous collection of men was beyond him. Soon after my arrival he decided that the Orderly Room was too noisy and fitted up a little office for himself down the road. More and more work devolved upon me, and soon, except for a few field-exercises, I was in fact running almost everything. I have never worked so hard for so long. There came a time when I knew more about the Regiment's Warrant Officers,

---

[1] Peniakoff (1897–1951) was awarded the M.C. and D.S.O., as well as French and Belgian decorations. See his book *Private Army* (1950).

Captain and Adjutant

N.C.O.'s and Guardsmen than anyone else, and I was constantly rung up by the Regimental Adjutant in London for information.

My day began by my taking a large drill-parade at 8 a.m. In peacetime the Adjutant always did this on horseback, but there were no horses now, and I took the parade in very expensive riding-breeches and boots, which occasioned some ribaldry among the junior officers.

The Training Battalion Officers
(Hugh Fraser on Colonel Tim's right)

All I had to do was to call the parade to order, with the R.S.M. at my side, and then walk round the squads to watch them being drilled by sergeants. One of Kirk's favourite ploys was, early in the proceedings, to have some incompetent man run off to the guardroom in arrest *pour encourager les autres*: he was later released with a caution. Also the R.S.M. was always trying to make me laugh by shouting out such remarks as 'Sergeant Snooks, that ginger-headed man in the rear-rank is walking like a PANSY'. Finally I dismissed the parade, changed, had breakfast in the Mess and began my long day in the Orderly Room.

Luckily I had a large and very efficient staff in a big office behind the Orderly Room, headed by O.R.Q.M.S. Ken Lockley, a young, intelligent, energetic man with a fine sense of humour. His predecessor had insisted that all the girl-clerks should sit with their faces to the wall, so as not to distract the male clerks from their work. Lockley asked me if this ridiculous rule could be cancelled, I agreed, and Lockley was soon courting the prettiest of the girls, whom he later married. He had a first-rate second-in-command called Harris, whom Lockley always teased by calling him 'Junior', and there was a female clerk of uncertain age, known and loved by all as Blossom. We were a very

The Orderly Room Staff
(Lockley on my right, his future wife behind us, Blossom and Harris on my right, Ernest Moss top left)

happy and trouble-free party. Thirty-four years after the end of the war I received, out of the blue, one of the nicest letters ever from former Guardsman Ernest Moss, saying how much he had enjoyed working for me in the Orderly Room. He was a great lover of opera, and when he found that the Slow March of the Coldstream was from *The Marriage of Figaro* he was immediately reconciled to the Army and slow-marched proudly forward, until he was recruited into the Orderly Room.

By tradition the Adjutant commanded the corps of drums, which was in fact run by the Drum Major, though culprits were marched before me for punishment. 'What has this man done, Drum Major?' 'Lost the button off his B flat flute, sir' in a high-pitched squeaky voice, and a suitable punishment was dealt out by me. All other culprits were marched before the Commanding Officer. After the R.S.M. and I had discussed the crimes and punishments, I told the Commanding Officer what to say. If a man whose crime we hadn't discussed was marched in, he had to be marched out again while Colonel Tim was put in the picture.

When the V.Is (doodle-bugs) began to come over there was a ter-rifying moment between the cutting-out of their engine and the

The Corps of Drums

explosion. I ordered the Orderly Room staff, directly they heard the cut-out, to hide under the tables, which would at least shelter them from flying glass. The V.IIs were less frightening, since one heard nothing before the explosion.

[2]

I had a large comfortable bedroom near the Mess, with Thatcher in attendance. The food in the mess was as good and plentiful as ever, and one day I asked the presiding genius Sergeant Callow how on earth he managed to maintain such a high standard. 'Well, sir,' he answered, 'I do sometimes wonder what the people of Godalming *do* for fish.' I questioned him no more.

With petrol-rationing ever stricter I decided to leave the car with Comfort in case of emergency, since Bromsden Farm was very isolated, and I bought two second-hand bicycles, on which Thatcher and I, whenever I had a clear week-end, rode to the nearest station, put them on a train to Reading, and pedalled home, up one very steep hill. I had heard that a Surrey town was asking people to remove bricks from a mass of bombed houses, so I hired a van and driver, who bought a vanload of bricks to Bromsden, and with them Thatcher built paths all round the garden.

Soon after the children got home they started going to the co-educational Homer school, which they reached by bicycle and bus. At the end of the year I reopened my little black notebook.

29 December 1943. Pirbright. Recently the children asked Comfort the following questions:
Bridget (nearly nine): 'Did you choose Daddy, or did Daddy choose you?'
C: 'I think we chose each other.'
B: 'Were you always as merry together as you are now?'
Duff ($7\frac{1}{2}$) Asked whether C would teach him to cook.
She said yes, she was all for boys being able to cook as well as girls.
Duff: 'Then if my wife died I could feed the children.'
2 January 1944. Pirbright. Home for twenty-four hours yesterday, and this morning took Bridget and Duff to church at Bix. It was the first time I'd been to church with them, and their first churchgoing in England. We went by bicycle, both of them looking very smart and sweet in grey flannel suits. Bridget looked very like a tiny edition of Comfort. The service consisted of nine carols, interspersed with brief lessons, the first five of which were read by children. Duff whispered to me: 'Shall we all get a read, Dad?' After each lesson the reader lit a candle, much to the children's pleasure. When we got to 'Good King Wenceslas' Bridget laid aside her book of words with a superior air and sang from memory. Both behaved beautifully and managed to hang on to their sixpences until the plate came round.

In the afternoon, bicycling to Reading *en route* for here, as I struggled in bottom gear at the top of an incline, a smartly dressed old gentleman with a silver beard and mad yellow eyes, who was walking the other way, shouted out: 'What price the Germans now? Pretty well bottled up!' Morale must be very high to penetrate to these levels.

In the train I started Richard Hughes's *A High Wind in Jamaica*, which I hadn't looked at since it appeared in 1929. Greatly taken with it once again. One of the pleasures of approaching forty is that one has had time to forget all but the general impression of books which one originally enjoyed before reaching what are known, rightly or wrongly, as years of discretion.

12 January. Pirbright. A day in London. Took Bridget and Duff to their first play, *Peter Pan.* First gave them and Diana Gamble lunch at the Guards Club. Duff was silently pleased and proud when I took him to the men's side to wash. He had never seen an upright urinal before, but quickly got the idea, and later in the theatre approached one as to the manner born. He looked very small and blond among a lot of tall officers.

They adored the play and discovered how the flying was done only at the very end. The theatre was full of children who were rapt at all action, but chattered through dialogue. Bridget and Duff leant forward, staring and thrilled. Occasionally Duff said: 'This *is* lovely,' and in the interval he had a serious debate with a little girl behind as to the difference between Acts and Scenes.

Afterwards saw them as far as Paddington and then came back here. At midnight I saw 275 men off to the Central Mediterranean Front, calling the roll in the dark, pushing men into railway carriages etc.

23 January. Drove over from Pirbright with two Guardsmen (a learner-driver and his instructor) and lunched at Greatham. Except for a brief afternoon visit in 1938 I hadn't been there since the halcyon days of 1927. While I was talking to Wilfrid Meynell in the library much of the old enchantment came over me. W.M. deaf and rather toothless, but wonderfully active and alert at ninety-one. Memory rather confused, but clearer regarding the long ago. Then I drove to Stopham church and stood godfather to the latest Barttelot. He was very vociferous, but despite all his efforts was christened Robin Ravenscroft. Then delicious food, champagne, and a comfortable bed in the home of Pat's parents. Walter was rather piano with a cold. Gave Pat £3 worth of savings certificates as a christening present for Robin.

[3]

In February Deirdre and her children came home in an aircraft-carrier. The voyage took three weeks, since from New York they had to go down to Virginia to pick up some aircraft and a lot of New Zealand pilots. On the voyage they lost £14 gambling: otherwise they were Guests of the Navy. They stayed at Bromsden Farm until Deirdre found a little house in a Sussex village.

24 April.   Pirbright.   Comfort recently took the children to a hill above Greys Court, from which there is a lovely view across a small valley. Duff was entranced with it and said: 'Oh Mum, it is beautiful – all green and brown, like a camouflaged bomber, sort of?' A week or two ago I asked him to throw a large stone out of the orchard into the wood (he throws very well). He said: 'I'm not the sort of person who throws stones into woods.'

6 June.   Pirbright.   D. Day [of the Allied invasion of Europe] was much like other days here, except that I took my portable radio over to the Orderly Room and we heard news all day – Eisenhower's speech five or six times. Great air of relief after weeks of tension and the constant drone and roar of our bombers in the sky.

9 June.   Pirbright.   To London in mid-afternoon. Went to a cocktail-party given by Deirdre and Mary Booker. Uncle Duff arrived, plump and urbane as ever. He recently flew back from Algiers with de Gaulle, and had been vainly trying to persuade Winston to recognise de G's provisional Government. He was very amusing imitating Winston saying: 'You'll do yourself a lot of harm, Duffy, by associating with this wicked man, this implacable foe of our country.'

Duff said that any three men in the street could settle this matter in five minutes – any three, in fact, except Winston, de Gaulle and Roosevelt. He also said that Winston cherishes a passion for the President (just as he does for Beaverbrook) and hates de Gaulle as a man hates a woman he no longer loves. He also said that he had tried to convince Winston that the notes the U.S.A. are issuing to our invasion troops are bad money, backed by no one, and bound to cause inflation. Winston would not agree.

21 August.   Pirbright.   Just back from a heavenly fortnight's sick-leave, spent at Blockley and Bromsden. Thatcher fitted up a carpenter's bench for Duff in the shed, much to D's delight. He now wants a vice. Did not at all enjoy my first day back here.

10 September.   Pirbright.   Yesterday afternoon I picked mushrooms and blackberries with the children. They were really more interested in catching flies for their 'museum' – a number of matchboxes stuck together. Bridget missed a fly and said: 'The trouble is they're so damn wary'. I rebuked her for this language, but was impressed by her choice of words. Her vocabulary has grown markedly since she read all Ransome's books. Must tell him.

Adam can stand alone for a second and can say 'bang' – a symbolic first word, perhaps, for one born in 1943.

In those days I was so busy that I had time to read nothing but thrillers and detective-stories, and when dear Veronica Wedgwood became Literary Editor of *Time & Tide* she arranged for all such volumes to be sent to me. My first review, over the name Norman Blood, appeared on 14 October 1944, and this gentle task I carried on regularly till 1959.

Sunday, 22 October.   Pirbright.   Yesterday we visited Bridget for the first time at her boarding school at Fairford in Gloucestershire. I got leave from Friday evening, and at 7 a.m. on Saturday Comfort, Duff and I set out by taxi to Reading. Comfort tried to dissuade Duff from coming but he insisted. Sure enough he was bored stiff before we reached Fairford at 11.15. He bounced about the carriage, groaning with boredom, and sat on our only good cup (for coffee), breaking it to bits. I told him to shut up and sit still. He said: 'Daddy, you're an acid old person'. Later I sharpened a pencil with a knife, and he said: 'You're not sufficiently civilised to sharpen that pencil.' However he cheered up when we passed an airfield near Brize Norton, and particularly enjoyed a crashed glider in a field.

We met Bridget in the street, looking blooming and very pretty. She took us to the school, and while Comfort talked to the headmistress, Bridget showed Duff and me all over the school, excitedly flinging open doors – 'Here's *another* lavatory!'

Then we walked to the Bull and had an excellent lunch with Deirdre and Susie. When the pudding came round Bridget was suddenly overcome by home-sickness and wept bitterly. Comfort consoled her, and she had pretty well recovered by the time we left at 2 p.m. I'm sure she's happy at the school, but I was much moved by the day, remembering my own early misery at boarding school.

29 October.   Pirbright.   Last night at home I slept with Adam, so that Comfort could get a ten-hour sleep in another room (which she did). He went to sleep in his cot, and an early attempt to wake up at 9.45 p.m. I thwarted by stroking the back of his neck till he dropped off. At 11.15 p.m. he woke with a vengeance, and I took him into the big bed with me. We both slept at intervals, and in between he sat up, reciting the words he knows – BANG, BUM, BOMBER, 'ITE (light), or patted me on the face and gave me very wet and slobbery kisses – also kicked me a good deal in vital spots.

At 3 a.m. he was so wide awake that I put on the light and gave him his picture-books. He turned over his favourite one (pictures of farm animals) and imitated their noises – MOO, MIAOU, BOW-WOW and a particularly engaging one for chickens. This performance was repeated at 6 a.m. when he woke for good. Felt rather dotty this morning, but A is so angelic that one could not feel aggrieved.

31 December. Bromsden Farm. Adam's christening at Bix Church. When he saw the vicar he said 'Dad-dy' – an unpardonable error. He cried when *quantities* of water were sloshed over his head, but once put down he stumped happily over to the door till the end of the service. His godparents were Diana Gamble, John Piper and Bunty Stewart-Brown, who was in France with the Fifth Battalion. [Both he and Walter Barttelot were killed there, and we later learned that in his will Bunty had left Adam £1000, to be paid on his twenty-first birthday – an act typical of his generous nature.]

[4]

The liberating year of 1945 opened with a fierce frost. Thick ice and snow on the square made morning drill-parades impossible. Each week I took pay to a company which was doing special training at Singleton in Sussex, and on the way back I visited Deirdre at her home near Pulborough and Pat Barttelot at Stopham, where I helped her to sort out Walter's kit.

Every week-end I managed at least twenty-four hours at Bromsden, and on 19 January I drove Duff to his first boarding school, St Andrews, near Pangbourne in Berkshire. We were both in a very emotional state, he with natural apprehension and I with memories of my own misery in my first days at Stanmore Park in 1917. I suddenly realised that anything I told him now he would remember for ever, but I couldn't think of anything to say. No moral precept or fatherly advice would do, and I was baffled. Finally, when we had almost reached the school I said: 'One thing you must always remember. A thousand pence equal four pounds, three shillings and fourpence. I didn't discover that useful fact until I was thirty, and it was very useful in working out authors' royalties. So don't forget it.' 'No, Dad,' he said in a choking voice. I left him with the headmaster, Bobs Robertson-Glasgow, a man as gentle and courteous with the boys as he was with the parents, but I drove home feeling wretched.

During Duff's first holiday he said: 'Do you remember what you told me in the car on the way to school?'

'Yes, I do.'

'Well, the other day the maths master set it as a problem.'

'Did you admit you knew the answer, or did you pretend to work it out?'

'I pretended to work it out.'

'You did right,' said I.

On 24 January I noted: 'Pirbright beautiful for the first time, under deep snow, every branch outlined against a yellow snow-foggy sky.'

Five days later it was still snowing, and twelve new officers arrived from Sandhurst and other O.C.T.U.s. I lectured them for an hour and a half. Goodness knows what I told them, but I had to lecture each new batch as it arrived, and I grew accustomed to the task. I was still very busy in the Orderly Room, working there almost all day.

On 7 February I recorded a *cri de coeur*: 'It is almost impossible to buy a toothbrush, a sponge, a comb, or a hot-water-bottle.' On the 10th I got home in a taxi, three trains, a lift, and a long walk – the last in a hailstorm. At Pirbright I played a lot of bridge in the Mess and the temporary homes of married officers who were living out.

3 March. Home by bicycle. Bought three soup-plates in a Reading junk-shop. Looked with Adam for eggs (which he calls wigs) in the orchard – his favourite sport.

10 March. Home yesterday by bicycle and train. Edmund Blunden and his Claire arrived from London, E bringing some rare items and manuscripts of his own. Next morning he was deep in Shelley's letters (my copy, his own being immured in Oxford). Thatcher laid a brick path between the lawn and the lavender, and I began to get the top winter-coat off the lawn with the mower.

After lunch the sun came out and we all sat on the lawn enjoying it. Adam stumped about stark naked and waving a fish-slice, which he calls 'ish-ice'. He is an enchanting little creature. Gossiped with Edmund and Claire. I am much happier about E, who is more serene and less nervous than I have ever seen him. Bicycled and trained back here with Thatcher.

[5]

Ever since Charlie left Bromsden in 1941 we wrote to each other as regularly as we could. He started in Liverpool, where he rashly became

Licensee and Manager of the Garrison Theatre Club, which soon collapsed. Thereafter he and Molly spent the rest of the war working in their two favourite places, Perth and St Andrews. In Perth they worked for their friend David Steuart in an established theatre, but in St Andrews they turned an old cow-byre into a tiny theatre, in which Charlie painted all the scenery, played all the main parts and stage-managed everything. He also wrote or adapted all their plays, from the Christmas pantomime to adaptations of *Cranford* and *Wuthering Heights,* and Shakespeare with all the sub-plots removed. As Charlie wrote: 'They'd make the professors spit blood, but my word the plays don't half biff on.' They were very short of male actors and in *Much Ado About Nothing* Charlie doubled the parts of Benedick and Dogberry.

They lived in a little flat near the Byre Theatre, worked day and night, and enjoyed it all immensely, as did the faithful audiences, who came to everything they put on. And then, in August 1946, Charlie's wife died, and on 26 September Charlie and Molly, after waiting for twenty years, were married in All Saints Church, St Andrews. They intended it to be a private affair, but some of their friends got wind of it and laid on a wedding-cake. At almost the same time a dotty old female relation of Molly's died and left her a snug little house at Milber, on the outskirts of Newton Abbot in South Devon, where they lived for the rest of their lives.

[6]

From Pirbright I several times visited Blossom in an Aldershot hospital. The poor old creature wept when she was told she'd have to stay there for two months.

The end of the war grew nearer and nearer as the Allied forces crossed the Rhine, and on the evening of 7 May the German surrender was announced on the radio. Next day was V.E. (Victory in Europe) Day, with a drumhead service of thanksgiving on the square. Afterwards I drove home in our renovated car. Flags everywhere, children's picnic and bonfire. Next day there was a general air of lassitude in the camp, but only five men were absent out of fifteen hundred.

The time had come for Hugh Walpole's executors to begin to dispose of his twenty thousand books and eight hundred pictures. My friend Dudley Massey, the head of the antiquarian booksellers Pickering & Chatto, helped me to sort the books in Christie's basement in Derby House and arrange them in lots. The first sale occurred on 28 May, and the rest were sold in five further sales, ending in July 1946. All six realised only £18,743 (less than a pound a volume) and they would certainly fetch a hundred times more today. At this first sale I bought five three-volume first editions of Thomas Hardy novels for a pound each.

We arranged for the pictures to be sold in three exhibitions at the Leicester Galleries, any that were left unsold to be auctioned by Christie's. Next day (29 May) I journeyed to Tonbridge for the wedding of Edmund and Claire – a huge spread afterwards and a very happy day.

Then I learned that 32 Stormont Road had been bought by a Wimpole Street doctor for £6250 – more than double what I had paid for it. Many years later when I was having a tooth out with a general anaesthetic, the anaesthetist, just before he plunged the hypodermic into my arm, said, in what sounded a faintly sinister voice: 'I once bought a house from you'.

I made several journeys to Stormont Road to pack up all that remained to be moved (Deirdre had taken her furniture long ago). Nellie and Amy very depressed, poor dears.

A new and very likeable friend made at Pirbright was a regular officer, Hugh Fraser. He was dark and skinny and much teased by his contemporaries. He loved telling a story against himself, of the time when he was a young officer. Totally unathletic but feeling he ought to take part in the battalion sports, he volunteered for a football match, which the Guardsmen were ordered to watch. He was stationed at full back when the ball rushed at him along the ground. He gave a tremendous kick, missed the ball altogether and fell face-first into almost liquid mud. As he got up, scraping the mud out of his eyes, he heard a Guardsman on the touch-line say to another: 'They call yon fooker Gandhi'. He had an estate in Jersey, and as soon as the Channel Islands were liberated he went over to see what damage the Germans had done, which was considerable. Years later I was instrumental in his selling the estate to Gerald Durrell for his Jersey Wildlife Preservation Trust, which still flourishes.

On 29 June there was a huge victory dance in the Mess, from which I got to bed at 0430 hours.

During the first week of August the Americans dropped atomic bombs on Hiroshima and Nagasaki. Japan surrendered and V.J. Day followed. Later in the month we took the three children for a fortnight to Tenby on the south coast of Pembrokeshire, where we stayed in a hotel and the children played happily on the wide sandy beach.

Back at Pirbright my Orderly Room duties were now principally concerned with repatriation and demobilisation, which was based on age and service. Some of my five years' soldiering had been gruelling and dull, but most of it I had enjoyed as a completely new experience which introduced me to many friends in all ranks. I had heard and seen no weapons discharged in anger except at aeroplanes and from the air, so I had been extremely lucky. My gratitude to the Regiment is endless.

Now, since I was thirty-eight I was released on 29 October, and after farewells to all my Pirbright friends I drove off, clutching my demob-kit, to rebuild my civilian life.

The Family, Summer 1944

APPENDIX A

Some Visitors to the fourth floor of 213 Piccadilly
1930–31

Actors & Actresses
Brian Aherne
Felix Aylmer
George Devine
Maurice Evans
Jean Forbes-
   Robertson
John Gielgud
Joyce Grenfell
Nicholas Hannen
Robert Harris
Jack Hawkins
Lewin Mannering
Cathleen Nesbit
Marie Ney
Laurence Olivier
Nigel Playfair
Ralph Richardson
Paul Robeson
Robert Speaight
Sybil Thorndike
Ann Todd
Veronica Turleigh
Diana Wynyard

Writers
Maurice Baring
John Drinkwater
Ashley Dukes
Ian Fleming
Peter Fleming
Graham Greene
A. P. Herbert
Aldous Huxley
Wyndham Ketton-
   Cremer
James Laver
Jim Lees-Milne
John Lehmann
Eddie Marsh
Charles Morgan
Raymond Mortimer
James Stephens
John Van Druten

Artists
Boris Anrep
Tommy Lowinsky
William Nicholson
James Pryde

Others
Richard Addinsell
Robert Birley
Duff & Diana
   Cooper
Charlie Marford

APPENDIX B

Five Letters from Robert Frost

5 January 1936   *3670 Avocado Avenue, Coconut Grove, Florida*

Dear Mr Hart-Davis, It has seemed to me too bad that my work couldn't have a broader chance in the country where it first found favor. What good boys those would be if they could get me going again over there. I am deeply touched by their friendliness. I have watched their young ways with jealous admiration, but the last thing I should have thought of was that they would be thinking of me. I seemed to play in luck in England for a year or two before the war; since then I have played in no luck at all. The publishing has gone by inadvertence. I let Longmans have that volume of my collected to please a young fellow who was acting as their agent. I didn't want them to have it. They didn't want it – and at least one or two others rather warmly did. London was in a winter fog, I was sick in bed with influenza at the time and the politics of poetry got to be too much for me.

If you are sure you want to try this restorative treatment, the first thing I suppose is for Richard Thornton of Henry Holt & Co to buy back the sheets he sold to Longmans and for me to pay Longmans back the three or four hundred dollars they advanced me. I don't remember what it was. I'll be glad to give it up. I hate advance royalties anyway and have never had any but these. I have no other foreign entanglements that I know of. Richard Thornton can tell you how my copyrights stand. I must have practically none. Which brings me to the question of how we could make the book you propose real property for you. What should you say to building it out from the Heinemann selection or the more recent Holt selection with material from the book I am to have with Holt this spring or autumn?[1] (Thornton thinks he can do better with it in the spring.)

---

[1] *A Further Range*, published by Harry Holt in 1936 and by Cape in 1937.

You see how many thousand miles (one and one half) from Amherst, Mass I am for my annual influenza.[2] I can't hope that you can be tempted down to the tropics to see us. I'm afraid I ought not to venture north right now. But it does seem as if I should have a talk with you. I like to be on personal terms with my publishers. What do you suggest? Of course if you advertised you had brought me to life again in England, I should have to be seen there in the flesh to bear you out. Whatever happens you have a lot of poets (Auden, Spender, Lewis and Engle) to thank for their good will toward me. And don't think I don't appreciate your part in this.

Sincerely yours   ROBERT FROST

17 January 1936   *3670 Avocado Avenue, Coconut Grove, Florida*

Dear Mr Hart-Davis, I'm still wishing I could see the whites of your eyes in these negotiations, so that I could judge for myself how much I might venture to get up my hopes. Well I must be content to rest in the assurance of your good letters. You and Mr Thornton may go ahead and settle my case between you. Don't let me scare you with any seeming over-concern. Experience has taught me to expect a good deal from publishers' magic. Still I am old and philosophical. I shall know how to take most of the blame for any book that doesn't come off.

Mr Thornton writes that you would probably use my Third Selection as a basis for your edition. We could cut that down a little to your price. The order is the chief thing to be kept. That is supposed to be an inspiration of about the amount of one poem.

Sincerely yours   ROBERT FROST

9 February 1936   *The Tropics*

Dear Mr Hart-Davis, I was wishing in my last letter that I could see you and satisfy myself of your being a fact. Such is my reversity – next trait to perversity. I am old and a joker. What I really meant was the opposite: I wished you could see me and on my countenance the pleasure you had given me by turning up and asking for me out of a clear sky. Unsought favors are about all that can please me any more. I sicken a little of procurement.

As to the rest of my letter I am dimmer. I have a feeling there was something in it you didn't quite understand. Probably some more

[2] I was in New York at this time.

American humor. I remember wanting you to know that while I do care, at the same time I don't care how our business comes out. Sales mean reputation and reputation still matters though not over much in comparison with several other things I could think up if I had to write an essay. You may or may not succeed with the book. Deep down in my heart I suppose I am sure you will. But no failure can take away from the delight of the Christmas present your first letter was.

Certain deeds of a fellow named Shanks[1] had about made me give up England. I trust he is no particular friend of yours. If he is I must hasten to add that I don't blame him too much. It is simply a manifestation of patriotism with him to feel that he must take sides with his Edward Thomas against me. I can always make allowances for patriotism. I could have amused you with the story had we met. The story can wait.

Sincerely yours   ROBERT FROST

Amherst Mass is my best address. In a few days now I shall be going to Harvard.

[Cablegram]   *1 June 1936*

BOOKS ARE YOURS AND SO AM I   FROST

11 July 1936   *South Shaftsbury, Vermont, U.S.A.*

Dear Mr Hart-Davis, Your letter takes the book and anything else of mine you ask for. We are both northerners. But as you are not north-temperate with me, so I will not be north-temperate with you. I had set my heart on your liking *A Further Range*. If you hadn't liked it, nobody else in England should have had it to publish. So you see how much hung on your favor.

Excuse the missing letter in favor and of course please see that my spelling is properly Anglicized for your editions.

I have reached an agreement with myself as to the omissions from my Selected. I trust the poor things not to feel there is anything invidious in their being left out. The list is subjoined.

Better not let me see the four prefaces to the book till they are in print. I don't want to seem in any sense to have dictated them. I must just leave them to you and fate. Four is a host. It is great fun mustering

---

[1] Edward Shanks, poet, journalist and author (1892–1953). I never knew him.

all the British critics inside the book. You're sure you're leaving anyone outside to review it?

And another thing. I believe I should like to delete the couplet in 'A Tuft of Flowers'

> 'I left my place to know them by their name;
> Finding them butterfly weed when I came.'

I was hardly more than a child when I wrote it, but it's a little *too* childishly awkward, and the continuity is all right without it.

You scare me with your invitation to come over so soon. We both want a good look at England again. But I fear Amherst College has claims on me for a while now that must be met. She sees me come back from Harvard a good deal the worse for being made of more than I deserved, and thinks she to herself, If he can exercise himself to be so pleasant to strangers, why can't he to the family? (She looks on me as one of the family, though I am no alumnus of Amherst or any other college.) The sight of me working hard in Cambridge made her realize what a fool she had been not to put me to work years ago. I wish the big book show came later. I suppose if you thought it worth the trouble I could run over and back on a fast boat. I should have to do it alone. It wouldn't be my idea of a happy or useful visit. Let's see what can be thought up.

Welcome the young son to this world for me. We might be embarrassed by the disorder he finds us in. But I know he wouldn't want us to stand on ceremony with him. Pinch his chin rather sharply for me and report carefully how he takes it.

Faithfully yours   ROBERT FROST

Poems to be omitted from my Selected

Twenty-five pages in all. A book goes forward with the poems marked for omission.   R.F.

16 January 1937   *947 West Agarita Avenue, San Antonio, Texas, U.S.A.*

Dear Mr Hart-Davis, Probably Richard Thornton has told you how sick I have been. Shingles and all that; so that I failed to rise to the occasion of the Harvard Tercentenary with an ode. Some suspect I was malingering to get out of a hardship. But I could admit it now if I had been. I can always own up in the end. No, I have been wretched. If the four prefaces to my Selected and the resultant sales in England make me famous enough to have a biography, I'm sure this year will figure in it as the year of my Great Disinclination. I have had spells of nervous intolerance before when my mood rejected everything I could think of to do. But this has been my worst. And I think the reason must be that I used up all my bravery in getting out two books, one with you, one here, and at the same time standing up to Harvard with those six brazen lectures. I don't know how I could face a firing squad in my present state. Or an audience. Or a batch of reviews from your newspapers. Or an income tax inquisition. Or you if you should turn up on this side and want to know why I hadn't written the letter due you for all you have done. To whomsoever I don't write, to you I must, if only to prevent the misunderstanding likely between two so far apart as we in age (fifty years, call it) in space (five thousand miles of land and sea) in language (according to H. L. Mencken) and in occupational interests (you the publisher, I the author).

What you are patiently waiting to hear when I shall get round to it is how I took your edition of my book. I am going to say I liked it regardless of whether it makes me sound modest or immodest. Two of the essays in particular should be good for my soul in that they extend my self-knowledge (somewhat). I am hoping all four will prove good for my reputation. I hate to be caught openly wanting anything I can't have. But I can confess to you privately I shouldn't mind having a British public for my works. Are you going to be able to get it for me? Don't feel too badly if you aren't. We'll stay friends just the same. You'll keep up what pressure you can for me and we'll pretend we are just biding our time with poems we both believe in.

Spare me the reviews. Give me your idea of the total effect. I'll take your word for it. I seldom see reviews unless they are very special and such as I should acknowledge. I shall want to thank Lewis, Auden, Engle and Muir. I wonder what their addresses are. I suppose I can reach them through your office. My address is 947 West Agarita Avenue San Antonio Texas USA. I have taken our vastest state to lose myself in this winter. Will you send me another contract here. I must have lost the first one if I ever had it.

I don't deny it is with mixed feelings I read what people say of me in prose. Muir for instance needn't have objected to the sententious repetition in 'Acquainted with the Night'. I wonder if he's sure I'm wrong there.[1] But never mind. You made me a charming book, and have given me all the chance I ask.

Ever yours   ROBERT FROST

---

[1] I'm sure Frost was right and Muir wrong.

ACKNOWLEDGEMENTS

I have been greatly helped by my sister Deirdre Inman, my son Duff, Diana Gamble, Paul Chipchase, Michael Bott, Keeper of Archives and Manuscripts in the University of Reading, Charlie Fitzherbert and Kate Grimond. My gratitude to them all.

For permission to print copyright material I am grateful to Professor Hamish Miles and the executor of Robert Frost.

I have consulted the following books:

The Coldstream Guards 1920–46 by Michael Howard and John Sparrow (1951)

Peggy Ashcroft by Eric Keown (1955)

Jonathan Cape, Publisher by Michael S. Howard (1971)

Peter Fleming, a Biography by Duff Hart-Davis (1974)

Peggy Ashcroft by Michael Billington (1988)

William Heinemann: a Century of Publishing 1890–1990 by John St John (1990)

INDEX